Over the many years I have worked in data analytics and business intelligence, the field has grown significantly. It's no longer enough to deliver accurate numbers and nice charts. We need to consider business value, governance, adoption, storytelling, and even corporate culture. Nicholas Kelly's new and essential book covers all that ground and more in a remarkably concise format. It is carefully thought out and brings real, practical experience to complex questions. The result is very clear, immediately useful guidance for strategy and tactics down to the details of dashboard design. But it's not one for your bookshelf—keep it on your desk.
Donald Farmer, Principal, TreeHive Strategy

For years professionals from around the world have sought out Nicholas Kelly's wisdom on how to have more impact at work with data analytics. At long last, Kelly has codified his wisdom in the book that you now hold in your hands. Achieving real business impact with data goes far beyond technical considerations—to achieve real, lasting impact with data you must focus on the human considerations. Through practical examples and real-world stories, Kelly has crafted a book that will teach you to capitalize on the human side of data analytics and deliver business-changing results.
David Langer, Founder, Dave on Data

When I look back at data-driven organizations, their leaders were super sensitive to numbers and hungry for information—but looking back doesn't help. Nicholas Kelly's book provides guidance on why insight mindset is important and how to build data-driven organizations. If you are looking to build an analytic capability or wondering how to improve one, this book covers the why, what, and how in a down-to-earth narrative. If you want to fast-track from lessons learned and get your program running from the get-go, read this book.
Akihiko Katayama, Chief Technology Officer, BaronsAI

Nicholas Kelly delivers in this practical guide to driving adoption of meaningful data analytics. Chock-full of stories that illustrate and humanize the life cycle, it is a must-read for the data analytics professional. If you want to know how to turn your data into impactful insights, follow the trail that Kelly has blazed.

Maria Massei-Rosato, Data Evangelist

Delivering Data Analytics

A step-by-step guide to driving adoption
of business intelligence from planning to launch

Nicholas Kelly

KoganPage

First published in Great Britain and the United States in 2022 by Kogan Page Limited

2nd Floor, 45 Gee Street
London
EC1V 3RS
United Kingdom

8 W 38th Street, Suite 902
New York, NY 10018
USA

4737/23 Ansari Road
Daryaganj
New Delhi 110002
India

www.koganpage.com

Kogan Page books are printed on paper from sustainable forests.

ISBNs

Hardback   978 1 3986 0297 7
Paperback   978 1 3986 0294 6
Ebook   978 1 3986 0295 3

British Library Cataloguing-in-Publication Data

A CIP record for this book is available from the British Library.

Library of Congress Cataloging-in-Publication Data

Names: Kelly, Nicholas (Director), author.
Title: Delivering data analytics: a step-by-step guide to driving adoption of business intelligence from planning to launch / Nicholas Kelly.
Description: New York, NY: Kogan Page Inc, 2022. | Includes bibliographical references and index.
Identifiers: LCCN 2021042710 (print) | LCCN 2021042711 (ebook) | ISBN 9781398602946 (paperback) | ISBN 9781398602977 (hardback) | ISBN 9781398602953 (ebook)
Subjects: LCSH: Business intelligence. | Business planning–Data processing.
Classification: LCC HD38.7.K45 2022 (print) | LCC HD38.7 (ebook) | DDC 658.4/72–dc23/eng/20211012
LC record available at https://lccn.loc.gov/2021042710
LC ebook record available at https://lccn.loc.gov/2021042711

Typeset by Integra Software Services, Pondicherry
Print production managed by Jellyfish
Printed in the UK by Henry Ling Limited, at the Dorset Press, Dorchester, DT1 1HD

This book is dedicated to my wife, Maria, who has been the most wonderful mother to our children and a life partner beyond my dreams. To our son, Aiden, who teaches me the importance of commitment and dedication. To our daughter, Athena, who reminds me not to take life too seriously and to always have a plan. I also dedicate the book to my parents, Aengus and Helen, thank you for all the years of support and patience. Finally, to my siblings, Douglas, Zoë, and Rachel, for all the memories we forged together growing up.

CONTENTS

ABOUT THE AUTHOR

Nicholas Kelly is the creator of the Enterprise Dashboard Process, the Dashboard Wireframe Kit, and the award-winning board game approach to BI requirements intake, the Dashboard Requirements Kit. He has numerous online courses and is a regular on the international speaking circuit.

He grew up in Cork, commonly referred to as the true capital of Ireland. Having lived in the Philippines and Singapore, he is now settled with his family in beautiful Bonney Lake on the west coast of the USA. His wife, Maria, and children, Aiden and Athena, enjoy regular excursions in their travel trailer and exploring the remarkable landscapes the USA has to offer.

During his career, Nicholas has been a management consultant to the world's largest organizations, helping them to act on their data, in a career that spans from Ireland to Singapore and the USA. From enterprise-grade ops dashboards for global banks with over 200,000 employees to intense demand, highly actionable, metrics delivery for Formula 1 drivers, he has developed a winning process for ensuring companies get ROI on their data via insight and behavioral change.

PREFACE

You are likely reading this book because you have struggled with how to increase adoption of data and insights. Indeed, you may have found you have done everything right and yet people are still slow to change their behaviors. The data quality is solid, performance is quick and responsive, and people can access the data when they need it, yet something is missing. There is a gap. The value is not there. The "So what?" is missing. People are just not leveraging data to make decisions. Like many, I stumbled into this problem not really knowing what to do about it early on in my analytics career.

It was my first day on the job, working for the most successful global analytics consulting firm in the world. I was big time. An Irish lad, born and raised in Cork, now standing in one of the tallest buildings in Singapore and gazing across at the Marina Bay Sands. With the opportunity to work with the brightest minds in the industry, I was both excited and incredibly nervous.

Being honest, I felt ill-equipped to fill the boots of the senior manager, data visualization role that I had been hired for. With a background in computer science, software development and user interface design, I had little exposure to analytics. My depth of analytics knowledge only extended to Google Analytics at the time. However, the biggest issues I was seeing did not seem to be addressed by technical expertise, or lack thereof in my case. Adoption kept coming up. People were the primary barriers to success, not just data. For the next several years I set about figuring out how to address and support adoption. First, how could I be more successful in driving adoption of reports and dashboards for my clients and then, second, could I teach it to others so they could be successful? Little did I know, but this path would lead me to designing dashboards for Formula 1 teams and high-pressure business environments for the C-suite.

This book is a distillation of that approach. From the years of experience as a consultant, with direct application in the real world, to the countless seminars and workshops where I have taught others how to apply the approach in their own careers, the book covers the wide range of applications and methodologies I have leveraged. To get the most out of the book, I suggest going to its website to access supporting materials and templates that will save you considerable time when implementing the contents within these pages.

www.deliveringdataanalytics.com

All "stories" in this book are for illustrative purposes only and do not represent any real events.

01

Insight mindset

The pace of analytics is fast. People want access to their data in short order and have the expectation that it is both not difficult, and that unnecessary barriers are put in place by the custodians of said data. Of course, neither of these positions is typically true, but they are perpetuated and compounded upon to the point that trust is eroded, and adoption of analytics suffers. There are many symptoms of this; one such example is a proliferation of dashboards and reports that are not used. They are created on an ad-hoc basis, for a narrow use case, and quickly lose value and become stale.

It can sound obvious, and it is, but we need to take a step we rarely take in the enterprise, namely, addressing the "So what?" If we surface such and such an insight, or piece of data, what impact will it have? If it will have an impact, is the organization ready for that impact? What are the change management implications of that impact?

The adoption struggle

To illustrate why this might be the case, imagine a burger that is about to be consumed. There is some data presented that illustrates the impact of the decision to eat the burger. By eating the burger, there would be a weight gain of 1.5lbs by Tuesday plus an increased risk of having a heart attack. This might sound like compelling data to make a case against eating the burger. It assumes weight gain is bad and that understanding the increased risk of having a heart attack is important.

Indeed, it assumes a great deal about what information the consumer would want to see.

However, what if this person is an MMA fighter who had a fight coming up on Friday and already had their weigh-in? They would want to put on as much weight as possible and really couldn't care less about the risk of having a heart attack.

Breaking this down further, the fighter is more interested in the weight gain by Friday, when the fight will take place, and not Tuesday. Also, that weight gain does not reflect past weight gain for eating similar food so the number itself is not trustworthy. Added to that, the increased chance of having a heart attack pales in comparison to the risks that a fighter faces. This data entirely misses the mark.

On the surface, the information presented seems like it would be insightful. It seems like there is value in knowing the weight gain and the risk of heart attack. However, without understanding the goals and desired outcomes the "end user" wants, it is very easy to miss the mark. As a result, if this were a dashboard, it would be added to the great unadopted reporting mountain that is ever-growing and always hungry for more.

Better understanding the goals of this individual will increase the likelihood that the presented data will be valuable and, ultimately, increase adoption. In so doing, the design can be reimagined. With the knowledge the end user wants to be in the best possible position to win their fight on Friday, the data they see must align with that goal. Reimagining what they need to see results in a new visual. The weight gain is still there but the day of the realization of that weight gain is now Friday, the day of the event.

However, far more important, is a new metric: how eating the burger impacts the odds of winning the fight. This is what the end user, the fighter in this case, truly cares about. That information was not freely available in the data, so it had to be derived. This is where value creation happens and where decisions can be influenced. Getting to this point requires several areas to align: user experience, change management, and analytics.

The moral of this story is that a report or dashboard can still fail to be adopted even if the traditional business intelligence (BI) steps are well executed, such as ensuring a high degree of data quality, enterprise-grade performance, and a well-designed report that the user can interact with.

Coming back to the enterprise, of course it is not as simple as the burger example, but the process is similar. That is, reports and dashboards are created with little or no understanding of the goals and business outcomes that are desired by the stakeholders. The BI developer operates in a silo, with little to go on in terms of requirements, and is expected to produce an output that will move the needle for the business. How can something of value be produced when there is little understanding of what value is? It requires a change in mindset.

Dashboard and reports—the data storefront

Delivering insight is a complicated business. There are many aspects to the data equation, including enterprise data warehouses, extract, load and transform (ELT), data catalogs, data quality, and performance. But it is in the interface that is presented to the user, the last mile as it were, where it all culminates. It is here where judgment lies. The intersection between data and those who will make decisions from it. The interface can take many forms. For the purposes of this book, the interface between data and people is assumed to be a dashboard and/or a report, and these terms will be used interchangeably. Great emphasis will be placed on this intersection, as it is the place most often ignored and where adoption is won or lost.

At the small scale, the approach can be applied to a single dashboard. At the other end, it can be leveraged as the operating model for an analytics center of excellence that shifts the data culture of an organization.

Build it and they will come (spoiler: they won't)

The 1989 movie *Field of Dreams* set a dangerous expectation in the area of business intelligence and analytics. The idea that if you build something, and do it well, that people will flock to it. The film purveyed a firm belief that if the design was good, the user experience exceptional, then users wouldn't be able to help themselves and adoption would be through the roof.

Many years of low adoption later, and that movie is considered heresy. A word of caution as you start this journey. Adoption is hard. Much harder than building dashboards and reports. Much harder than telling stories. Much harder than performance tuning and responsiveness. Even much harder than user acceptance testing (UAT) and training. It will stretch you and demand persistence. But, if you follow the steps in this book, you will have a far greater potential for greatly increasing adoption. So, buckle up, turn off the movie, and let's get to it!

Supporting decision-making

In the purest form, the desire is to use data to support and/or influence decisions. It is implicit that it is a good idea to do this, i.e., a change is needed from business as usual. The key word is change. Let me say it again. Change. Ask a change management expert and you will be told that change is hard. Change takes time. Ask a BI expert to build a dashboard (assuming all the data is in place) and you will be told it could be done in days. There is something funny going on here.

A dashboard, or report, if it does what it is designed for, is a change agent. A vehicle for creating a ripple in the organization to improve profitability, improve outcomes, improve performance, etc. On the one hand, a change agent can be launched in a matter of days or weeks, yet organizational change can take months to years. How can these two timelines be reconciled? The answer to that is, they are usually not reconciled. Yet it can be difficult to diagnose the problem as such. It is another log on the fire of low adoption of data.

STORY

I was on a call with a prospective client, talking through the process of building dashboards. There was good alignment on the approach and how business value was a priority for anything that would be created. Towards the end of the call, I was asked how long does each iteration of a dashboard process take? Being deliberately provocative, I said about three months. You could almost hear the person on the other end of the call spitting out his coffee. "*What!* Three months? We iterate every week, sometimes even daily! Why is it so slow?"

My response was to remind the prospective client why they had engaged with me in the first place—to increase adoption of their dashboards. Speed of iteration was certainly important, but adoption is the most important outcome of all. After some discussions, the consensus was that they would rather have one high-value, high-adoption dashboard versus ten that would sacrifice value for speed.

Change takes time. It is easy to throw around terms like "make decisions with data" or "actionable outcomes". To make those terms come to life involves people. People need to be brought on a journey for change to be effective. This is the true storytelling expertise that is needed.

It is not optimal to suddenly drop in a change agent amongst a bunch of people and expect perfect alignment and an immediate shift in decision-making. Try to recall instances where impactful change happened in a short amount of time. Change typically involves some mixture of discomfort and it can take time before acceptance and advocacy have an effect.

Change is not needed for business as usual. Leveraging data to influence or complement decision-making could very well involve change. So, it is better to assume a degree of change will occur versus not planning for it at all. Unless the idea is to not provide impactful data.

It sounds flippant, but if the idea is to not have a change impact, then why provide a feedback mechanism with data in the first place? Expecting an impact allows us to prepare for managing that impact, to deliver value and maximize adoption. Therefore, whatever process is followed, it must effectively bring people on a journey of change, so they feel like they are part of the story and not that the story is happening in spite of them.

Managing the experience

In a perfect world, assume the change impact is being adequately managed, there is a wonderful change process in place, and there is limited friction for people to make decisions. However, the user interface looks bad, and the user experience is frustrating. Everything could have been perfectly executed from a data quality and change perspective but there are still significant barriers as the user does not want to interact with something that has a poor user experience. Indeed, it can greatly erode trust and damage the data culture. Recall the burger example and the before and after. There can simply be too much information presented or the user might have to dig too far. Maybe the key information is buried in a tab or the colors and font are a mess. Basically, the interface is ugly and unintuitive.

Creating a positive user experience combines elements of user research, user interface design, data visualization, and more. Some, or all, of these terms may not be a strong suit for you. They are vital aspects of an adoption process. Curiously, user experience is a highly leveraged field in software development yet, in BI and analytics, it is somewhat of an undiscovered country.

What is user experience (UX)? It is the perceptions and responses a person has when interacting with a system, in this case a report or dashboard.

A positive user experience has many elements and each of these pillars is a field of study in itself. However, this is far too much detail for what is needed here but it does serve the purpose of showing that it is a very mature field and there are many rabbit holes one can explore.

STORY

Over the years I've had the opportunity to see what have been the most significant behaviors or actions one can take to have the largest impact on adoption. What I have seen is almost never directly related to data quality, like one might expect. Data quality can certainly be a component of low adoption but there can be high adoption with poor data quality. That is to say, good data quality is not a prerequisite for proceeding; indeed, if that were the case, a great many dashboards should never be created.

The biggest drivers of impact I have seen are when applying basic user experience principles. By basic I mean actually talking to people. User research. Certainly, where organizations already conduct interviews when building products (dashboards) then it is much less of an "Ah ha" moment. But in many organizations, the notion of conducting user interviews is so novel it can even border on the forbidden. It can seem so innocuous and trivial, but can often be revelatory in impact. "What do you mean, the user has never opened the dashboard?", or "They are using a version that is from last year, with old data?" are some of the gems that come up in user interviews.

Since time and resources are not infinite, a judicious selection of UX methodologies is necessary and must be tailored to be specific to BI and analytics. Any process focused on adoption must include talking to people. In a field with our fair share of introverts, the prospect of human interaction can seem a little daunting, but it is a vital linchpin in the journey of adoption.

As you can see, there are areas that affect adoption outside the four pillars of data volume, variety, velocity, and veracity. There are several pieces to the puzzle of delivering value. At a high level, there are three areas of confluence: data/analytics, change management, and user experience. This is the virtuous path to high adoption. Of course, very few people are experts in all three areas. Indeed, each area has tremendous depth and a vast body of knowledge. So how can one become competent in these three areas?

Great depth is not required, but a surface understanding is necessary. However, coupled with a step-by-step process, knowledge gaps can be overcome, in lieu of experience. Nothing can beat experience, but an impactful start can be made by following a process. Before understanding what such a process might look like, a mental shift is needed in how to approach creating value.

The value mindset

It is incredibly easy to get locked into the day job, the regular 9-to-5, and take it for granted. Going through the usual motions of the day, replying to emails, attending meetings, and hoping to find some time to do some actual work at some stage. The point is, we can get in a mental rut where we stop thinking strategically. A barrier forms that blocks higher-level thought, preventing us from stepping back to ask "So what?" What is the impact if this dashboard is created? The usual approach is to just dive in and start building.

It is a recipe for low adoption, and it starts with the mindset. The shift needed can be a subtle one, but it is truly impactful. To illustrate this, consider a basic sales process. An individual has a problem, a seller has a product that will fix that problem, the value of that product is conveyed to the potential buyer by the seller, and the individual buys that product from the seller because it will address their problem. This applies even for the lowest cost products. Yet, in the enterprise, where the costs are far greater, the value positioning can be lacking.

Expand that further into the enterprise. A marketing director would like to see the impact of her most recent marketing campaign. She makes a request of the IT department for a dashboard that can help her see the numbers. To make this request, she fills out an IT ticket. There is a single box in the form for the "description of problem." She fills it out:

> I need a way to see what's happening with my marketing campaigns and how they are performing.

This request makes its way to a BI developer in the IT department and the above description is all they have to go off. Heaven forbid they reach out to the marketing director for a conversation! No, they must forge on and invest 100+ hours in building a report that will address that very vague request.

Two months later, the marketing director receives an email with a link to a new report and, lo and behold, it sucks and is entirely unhelpful for what she needs. Indeed, her marketing campaign is already finished and she has moved on to other things. She is unhappy, another redundant report has been added to the scrap heap and hours of effort have been wasted. No value has been created.

The cost of this approach can be quantified in a number of ways. One such is a basic hour's estimation. The BI developer might have a fully burdened cost to the organization of $50/hour. Even assuming just 100 hours were spent on this effort, it comes to $5,000. That's $5,000 for no value. However, it's worse than that. Trust has been further eroded.

It is a scenario that is all too common, yet entirely avoidable. If the BI developer had a value mindset, the scenario might go something like this. The BI developer receives the ticket, reads it, and finds it is lacking in detail. There is no defined business outcome. Indeed, there is nothing in the ticket that would help him understand the "Why?" Bucking the trend, he does something unconscionable—he sends an email to the marketing director asking for a meeting.

Dear Jane

I have just received your request for a marketing report and I'm excited to handle this request for you. I've proactively placed a meeting on your calendar for early next week so we can discuss your vision and the outcomes you are seeking, so I can make sure I am going to focus on your goals as well as to check the speed you need. Please see the proposed agenda below and feel free to change as desired:

Goals and objectives

What does a successful report do for you?

Timing (refresh rate and when you need the report)

Next steps and what to expect

Thank you and looking forward to working with you.
John
BI Developer

Since John has a value mindset, he will not start any development until he has met with his "client" and covered the areas outlined in his email to Jane. John understands that the IT ticket is just the start of the process of value creation, more of a request for a conversation, but certainly not the last word in gathering requirements. Indeed, after having the conversation with Jane, John might find that it is not possible to do what Jane is requesting and, rather than taking two months to deliver a report that misses the mark, he can directly let Jane know. Disappointing? Yes, but so much better than the alternative. Regardless, trust is being built, even without value creation.

On the flip side, John might be able to get close to what Jane wants and produce something of value to her. In that scenario, Jane is happy, value is created, and trust is built.

It is a simple example, but it illustrates how taking a different mindset can dramatically change how reports and dashboards are produced. By itself, it requires a little mental fortitude. Out of the gate, very few individuals would take this approach without specific training or following a certain process. Partnered with a process, a value mindset becomes second nature.

The product mindset

A value mindset is the precursor to a second necessary shift, a product mindset. An understanding of why products exist and how to sell them. The BI or analytics team is creating data products and these products must have value to their market, i.e., the end consumers of the data product.

The path to understanding value is to understand the needs of the intended buyer. What benefits do they need to realize for them to buy? It is truly no different in the enterprise. For a businessperson to regularly spend their time and energy on a dashboard, they must realize the benefits of doing that. Such benefits might be time savings, increased sales, reducing risk, etc. To interpret those benefits, there is a need to put on a salesperson's hat. Sales can be broken down simply as identifying the problem, highlighting the impact of the problem, identifying the benefits if the problem was not there, and what the cost of the solution is. The cost is only presented after the benefits are identified.

Creating reports and dashboards requires a sales mindset. There must be a focus on what the benefits are to the end user. If the user adopts it, what benefits will they realize? Adoption happens before the dashboard is built. Adoption is a done deal before a line of code is written. That is why thinking of a dashboard in the same way as you think of a product can be a game-changer.

By taking a product mindset it forces a focus on benefits. What if your life depended on selling something? The natural next step would be to find out how sales work. What is the very best way to sell something? In the example above, the "long form sales letter" approach was being used. In that case, it was delivered in a face-to-face interaction. Alternatively, one would come across the long form sales letter in a newspaper or on websites. However, it does require extended attention during a single interaction.

So how does this work in the enterprise? First, we must explore the modern sales approach to products.

These days, product sales happen over a sequence of interactions. It is a sequenced version of the long form sales letter delivered in bite-sized chunks over a set period. A great example is a product launch. Imagine a new BI training course is being created. The process starts with understanding the needs BI professionals have. What are the gaps in their knowledge? What are the benefits of addressing those gaps? With that understanding, a product launch plan can be devised with a launch date in mind—let's take six weeks as an example.

Weeks one to three might involve messaging the potential buyers about what their biggest pains are and how they can be solved, at a high level. Week four might give a deep dive into solving one of them. Week five would let them know there is a course being launched that is going to address all their pains. The week of the launch would have some special offer or discount if they buy immediately.

That is a very compressed overview of how sales can work. A series of touch points that establish what the pains are, how they can be solved, and what the benefits are.

A typical story in the enterprise could be elevated by taking a product mindset. A BI team is tasked with building a new report. The team thinks of a report as a product they need to create. Now, a product must be valuable. It must convey benefits to whoever is going to buy it. The BI team first seeks to understand what the benefits are by gathering more detailed requirements and establishing the value proposition of what they are going to build. Then they can effectively sell their product to the end user with the knowledge that it is addressing some, or all, of their pains.

When starting a new dashboard, with the intent of selling it, it absolutely requires a different approach to business as usual. The mental shift is vital, but only becomes impactful when partnered with a process. A successful process must have the sales journey built into it.

The elements of a process

There will always be individuals that spot deficiencies and will take proactive steps to address them. A natural ability to navigate the corporate waters to find a solution and still be able to deliver value. Many systems exist, both natural and human-made, to ensure there is alignment between what is desired and what results.

Consider the stages of the typical process. There is limited input from the stakeholder, e.g., Jane fills out an inadequate IT ticket. Input being the first stage of this process. Then, in short order, creation begins, with very limited direction. At the end, the result may be useful for the stakeholder, but it likely will only be a shadow of what it could have been.

In this scenario, there was an input stage and a creation stage. Albeit a very limited input stage. There is a key element missing in this basic process. One that is evident in many natural systems, indeed, it can be vital for not just survival but also to thrive. Feedback. Feedback is the linchpin of value creation. It must be fast, and it must be frequent. Without feedback, John goes off on his own, into the murky shadows of the IT department, and only surfaces again weeks later with the completed report. It is the first time Jane can give feedback, which is somewhat useless at the end of the process.

Jane might give very useful feedback, but it could involve doing a bunch of re-work and cost additional expensive development time. Not only that, but it is likely to frustrate Jane as she now has to wait longer to get the information she has been looking for. Of course, John is bothered by this too and no one comes out happy with this process. It may sound burdensome to have frequent check-ins, but it is far preferable to dealing with the fallout from a more traditional waterfall process.

To be effective, a process must have frequent, and iterative, cycles of input, feedback, and creation. This level of simplicity must be maintained, even when working with topics as complex as data science and machine learning. If the output is going to be used by a human, this fidelity of process is needed.

The term "iterative" is a key element in a process. It allows for imperfection. It allows for improvement of the process over time. Rarely is it possible to suddenly introduce an entirely new process and expect it to be all followed from day one.

STORY

Over the years I have explored well-established methodologies and frameworks that support adoption, such as change management, user experience, process improvement, agile methodologies, and others. A term that jumped out at me was "the art of distraction." In order to implement a new process, which can be a high-friction journey, one can leverage a means of distracting from the large change, so people are not focused on it.

While working with a utility client, I had an opportunity to see it in action. The client was well-versed in change and also ran a BI team. She wanted to introduce the process in this book but knew it was not going to be easy. Her plan was to not talk about process, but instead to make it all about playing a business board game. She used the Dashboard Requirements Kit, a fun tool I had created for conducting requirements gathering, and said to her team of BI developers

"Today we are going to learn how to play a board game!" during a half-day training.

Implicit in the board game was the process that must be followed, but no one was talking about that. They were excited about this new thing they had. It allowed them to show up to their stakeholders and have a discussion about this kit and how using it would help design a dashboard. They were already adopting a best practice process for analytics adoption without the stakeholders focusing on it.

Last time I checked, some years later, they were still using it.

So, what should a process include?

- A value-oriented approach.
- A product and sales launch sequence.
- An agile and iterative methodology.
- Aspects of change management.
- User research and aspects of user experience methodologies.

This is the process that will be elucidated in this book, along with an explanation of how it can be used in the fast-paced enterprise environment. In addition to that, the approach is designed with the understanding that a range of personality types may be tasked with executing the steps in this book. People who may be uncomfortable talking to others. People who have no interest in thinking about value and product sales. It is all wrapped into the process. However, it does require a strict adherence to the approach. Perhaps not all at once, but over time, all the steps should be followed to have maximum impact.

Following the approach will result in transformation not just for the business and the people you and your team interact with, but also for the people leveraging the process.

Shifting the data culture

If getting people to act on data was easy, you would have probably done it already. For better or for worse, data is the relatively easy part of this equation:

$$Data + people = value$$

The promise of data has been an easy one to talk about. It is the people part of the equation that is hard, especially since there is little attention given to enablement in the data world. It is almost assumed that people will act on data if it is available. Ultimately, for the vision of BI and analytics to be realized, there needs to be a cultural shift in the organization. Setting that as the wider goal becomes the North Star. Whether you are early in career or a senior executive, you can further that cause by leveraging the steps in this book.

A note on self-service

For the sake of clarity, it is important to identify what role self-service has. It is the opinion of this author that a significant demand for self-service was born from the "business" not getting access to the data they wanted from the IT, BI, or analytics functions. If that problem is addressed, then a large argument is removed for having a pragmatic system in place to govern it. Indeed, just unlocking self-service in a large organization can lead to a massive proliferation of ungoverned reports and dashboards. It truly becomes an unwieldy beast to manage.

That being said, there will always be a group of people who want to get into the data directly themselves and it is certainly appropriate not to constrain them. But, for most people, if their data requirements are appropriately addressed, at a reasonable speed, then the clamoring for self-service should greatly reduce.

Another consideration is that many self-service requests can be misguided. They do not result in value and meaningful impact. What if they are not aligned to the goals of the organization? What if they pull numbers that don't agree with other reports? There are many areas for concern.

There is a happy medium. The approach in this book lends itself to handing over responsibility for some of the steps to others. It is quick, iterative, and transparent. It is designed so that non-technical people can be involved. All steps can be traced back to previous steps. A BI developer can immediately understand who the dashboard is being designed for. A business leader can jump in and see what questions this dashboard will be answering and why.

With that out of the way, let's talk about strategy and planning.

02

Strategy and planning

I was on my way to a requirements gathering workshop I was going to deliver in Jakarta. It was going to be a typical session of aligning the participants on the goals of a specific dashboard and who it was being designed for. By the end of the full day session, we would walk away with the requirements necessary for building a vitally important operational dashboard.

As always, I arrived early so I could prepare the workshop space, and make sure the catering was in place and all the materials were where they needed to be. It was going to be a productive session, perhaps a little tricky to manage as there were going to be approximately 40 attendees, but I'd certainly run workshops with more.

I started to get a little concerned, when at 8:50 a.m., ten minutes before the start time, no one had wandered into the room yet. By 9:00 a.m. there was still no one there. At about 9:15 a.m., all of three people had come in and sat down. Was it me? Did I not send out the calendar invite? Did I miss something? Sitting down and chatting to the three people there, it turned out I did miss something. Something big. And it was entirely my fault.

More on this later.

The start of the process

A new dashboard has been requested. There is scant detail and information. Where do you start? The first steps are the most important, and any well-executed journey has a plan. More than a plan, there is a strategic vision for the undertaking. For a typical project, that can be broken down into these main areas:

1 • The intended goals.
2 • The desired outcomes.
3 • How will these outcomes be achieved?
4 • Who are the people involved?
5 • When will it be released?
6 • Who and what will be impacted?

They do seem like common sense, but this is the first step that is often missed and can have significant impact to adoption down the road. Let us explore each of these in more detail.

The intended goals

The goals answer the "Why?" Why do we need to do this? In a more tactical sense, assuming there is a resulting interface that the end users will interact with, what is the business impact that will result from those interactions?

Goals are very easy to get wrong. Quite often, they are misinterpreted as things that need to happen, like "automate ETL (extract, transform, load)" or "improve data quality." They are not goals. Goals should be visionary statements like "increase sales." The adage "What is measured is what is managed" starts here. Value creation starts at the inception.

When diagnosing why data initiatives often do not get adopted, a common reason is failure to create business value. If that value is not clearly stated at the beginning, then it is highly unlikely to ever be attained. It becomes more about chance value creation than a strategic plan.

Value by chance is not ideal because it may not be aligned to the wider company strategy.

It is for these reasons that goals must be set that have a clear and transparent alignment to the organizational strategy and how those goals can be realized through individuals making decisions with the data that will be made available. There is a clear value chain from company strategy right down to the individual employee that will be interacting with the data. Naturally, this is easier said than done, but if it was easy then everyone would be doing it already. However, it is the first step that must be taken to pave the way for success down the road.

The desired outcomes

Where goals are visionary in nature, outcomes are measurable. Extending the goal of "increase sales" from above, a measurable outcome could be "increase sales by 15 percent within one year." It is specific and timebound. Naturally, it must be tightly coupled with the goals. The goals must be aligned with the overall business strategy. Any wavering here will cause greater misalignment further down the value chain.

This integrity of value must be maintained all the way through to the charts and key performance indicators displayed on the dashboard. Thereby, the people looking at the dashboard and taking actions are doing so to further the vision and goals of the business.

It is rare in the enterprise that such attention is given to the inception of a new dashboard. However, it is also little wonder that many dashboards fail to deliver value and on the promise of how data can transform an organization. By making this a step in the process, it acts as a forcing function to ensure the stakeholders are giving it the attention it deserves. For data to deliver on its promise, people need to engage and play an active role in shaping the outcomes.

A common frustration for data professionals is the unrealistic expectation from businesspeople on how quickly a data project can be turned around. In addition, with very little engagement, the data professional is expected to be able to deliver value. This early step is designed to increase engagement and to have greater ownership of the outcomes from the business. It drives agency and accountability because the business needs to think how they are going to achieve the outcomes.

Achieving the outcomes

Pearson's law: "When performance is measured, performance improves. When performance is measured and reported back, the rate of improvement accelerates."

This short quote is from Karl Pearson, a statistician who studied Albert Einstein's work. It rings true because it assigns accountability. But accountability without feedback can mute improvement. To succeed, there must be both a mechanism for measurement and for feedback, hence the reporting piece.

Considering the intended outcomes is a positive start, if not a bit of wishful thinking. However, working through how they are going to be achieved and measured can be sobering. Yet this is what must happen to ensure a successful dashboard is being built. Again, it is the continuation of the value chain. One break in the chain and it cascades to a less valuable dashboard coming out the end.

Achieving outcomes requires action. Action that is going to move the business closer to the desired outcome. Any action that is not so aligned should not be included—it dilutes the focus and impact the dashboard can have.

STORY

Back in Jakarta...

It was not a good day for me. There had been three months of preparation work and build-up for this workshop. It was not just because there was lots of work to do beforehand, it took that amount of lead time to get 40 people scheduled and able to attend a half-day's time investment in a workshop.

It was my fault. I had failed to understand the people involved, especially the politics of this particular organization.

Many are familiar with, and have experienced, the traditional divide between IT and the business. The business doesn't like IT because they are perceived as slow and always say no to requests, hence the advent of self-service. IT is frustrated with the business because they always throw last-minute requests and often fail to give adequate context. There are valid points on both sides of the fence.

It was this friction, and the degree of it, that I had not anticipated. Here is what I later understood to have happened. All the intended participants had been sent a meeting invite for the workshop. Indeed, there was an abundance of communication in the lead-up to the event where there was ample opportunity for people to see who was going to be attending. The IT people saw names of people they very much disliked from the business and business folks saw the typical names from IT they perceived as blockers and nay-sayers.

The business attendees felt it was just going to be a waste of time since IT was going to be there. The IT people expected it was a trap and a way for the business to steamroll what they wanted through, in front of a large group. Most attendees had made up their minds that they would not be going. They had made that decision weeks ago and just ignored subsequent communications about the event.

It was very much a people problem, and a significant learning for me.

The people involved

For any strategy to work, an understanding of the players involved is necessary. The truer this understanding, the more likely that a plan can be executed against a strategy and ultimately achieve the intended goals. A typical data effort will have a mix of people or roles involved:

- stakeholder
- end user
- executive
- data owner
- data engineer
- BI developer

- data scientist
- consultant
- project manager
- business analyst

Consider that a person and a role are interchangeable and there can be overlap. For example, a data engineer may also be playing the role of a business analyst. A BI developer may also be an end user. Or an end user might be a stakeholder and an executive.

With many roles comes the potential for misalignment, disagreement, and friction. It is a risk, if left unmanaged, that can easily derail any data effort. People will find myriad ways to have conflict, to feel hard done by, and/or cheated. Many times, these feelings are justified! To manage that risk, alignment must be sought at the inception of the project.

There needs to be a unifying vision that is going to bring all these roles together. To rally behind a common cause. To have consensus around how to execute against that vision while having a realistic understanding of the scale and nuances of the problems and challenges. To achieve this, we need a strategy.

The stakeholder

Some of these roles will be familiar and some may need further explanation. Starting with the stakeholder, this is the driving force behind this effort, be it a dashboard that is being created or some other data project. The stakeholder can be identified in several ways. Do they control the budget? Do they have authority to start or end the project? Will they directly benefit from the project? It can be just one of those to identify a stakeholder.

STORY

While speaking at a conference on this topic, a member of the audience, let's call her Sarah, said she was struggling to identify the stakeholder for a dashboard she had been tasked with building. She sits in IT and requests come in through a ticketing system. Basically, all she had to go off was an IT ticket that requested data related to marketing performance for a large marketing campaign that had recently launched.

The ticket made no mention of any names, people or roles that needed this dashboard. This was normal stuff for Sarah. She would just put her head down and get to work on developing the requested dashboard with this deeply limited amount of context.

It was a lengthy conversation. I asked her if she ever received any feedback after she delivered a dashboard through the ticketing system and she did not. It was basically a black box. No communication in or out. And that was seen as a good thing! Created by design to have an efficient system for supporting ticketing requests. Sarah worked for a very large and deeply siloed organization.

For Sarah, talk about stakeholders and end users was entirely novel. Even though the system was not designed for this, she was eager to find a way to make this new approach work for her and she asked me how, in spite of how her organization worked, could she follow this approach?

First, we looked at what was lacking. There was no vision, no desired outcomes being sought, and no understanding of who this was being designed for. However, there was a lead we could follow. Clearly there was the desire to see the impact from a recent marketing campaign. So, who would want to see that? There could be a few candidates—possibly sales but more likely it would be marketing. Why? Because sales doesn't need to justify marketing spend or to prove return on investment on marketing dollars spent. We assumed it was marketing making the request.

Based on that assumption, if correct, there were a few more conclusions we could draw. While the request for this ticket was probably made by the person who ran the marketing campaign, the stakeholder was probably their boss or a few levels above them, depending on the size of the marketing. We first had to identify the stakeholder as value cascades from that individual. The first easy port of call was to ask the question "If this marketing campaign was successful, who would benefit from that?" Certainly, the person who ran the campaign but also whoever was the head of marketing. Sarah didn't know anyone in marketing. I could see how unnatural this process seemed to her, but she was very eager to push through her discomfort and continue the discussion.

We determined her next steps, and this is where the real discomfort lies, especially for someone in Sarah's situation who had never done this before. The aim was to find out who was the head of marketing and try to understand them better. Could Sarah spend 15 minutes with them to have a conversation about the vision for the marketing campaign?

If Sarah could understand the vision, she could build a far more valuable dashboard. Conversely, she might find that there is insufficient data available to build a dashboard that aligns with the vision and she could save herself some time.

All of this was somewhat revolutionary for Sarah's organization, but she was committed to making it work. I later heard back from Sarah—she wanted to share what had happened. She had found out who the dashboard requester was, a marketing manager running a campaign for a specific product. The product was not even mentioned in the IT ticket! Sarah had a chat with this manager and ended up having great engagement and tailoring the dashboard to be very specific to the need. The ultimate stakeholder was the marketing director, and, through the manager, Sarah was able to infer the objectives and vision of that director.

This had transformed Sarah's enjoyment of her role and produced far more value to the marketing manager. Sarah would now look at an IT ticket coming in as the start of the journey, a mystery she needed to solve to find out who she needed to talk to, to better understand the request.

The stakeholder may be a user of the dashboard, but they also might not be. There can be overlap. A stakeholder might just be interested in a higher level, or strategic, view of the dashboard being created. Ultimately, the stakeholder needs to provide the vision and alignment with organizational goals. The stakeholder defines value. They bring the strategic perspective and desired outcomes.

The end user

The most obvious way to identify the end user is to specify the person or people that will be interacting with the dashboard that is to be created. They are the ones that open the dashboard on a Monday morning to understand what is going on with their business and what they need to do. They take the actions that move the business along the path in alignment to the vision and outcomes identified by the stakeholder.

Any visual, chart, or key performance indicator (KPI) that the end user sees on this dashboard has a place and purpose in the production of value. While the stakeholder identifies the value chain, it is the end user that gives it life and enacts it based on what they are seeing on the interface.

There is some caution needed. An end user must be carefully identified. Recall the burger example. The reason it was effective, and valuable, was through a narrow identification of what motivated that end user. In that case, the end user was anyone who was an MMA fighter with a fight coming up soon.

STORY

Early on in any data project, it is vital to understand the scope of how many end users will be interacting with an interface. On one such project, I was asked to support in establishing the end user goals. There were about 2,000 end users identified. It is best to never assume similar motivations and goals for an end user population. With that in mind, I set about better understanding this group of people.

After some discussion with the stakeholders, a few interviews with various end users, and a reassessment of the desired value, it was clear there were many competing goals amongst this group. Indeed, any dashboard presented to this group at large would likely be dissatisfactory for a large swathe of them. They had differing goals and challenges they needed to solve.

I set about grouping together similar goals and challenges as a way of defining subsets of the end user population. What resulted was five groupings, or personas (more about these later). Essentially, five different dashboards would be needed to provide enough value to these people while maintaining a balance in not going to the other extreme and creating a dashboard tailored specifically to each of the end users. With these five groupings we could still ensure the value-chain was intact. However, less than that, and it could be a challenge.

The end users are the most important part of the adoption equation. They are at the vanguard of adoption. It is why great care must be taken in selecting and identifying the end users. Who are they? What are their goals? What is their week like and how can the dashboard help them?

The executive

Any work with data will usually involve a wide range of people and roles. One of those roles that is least likely to be directly involved is the executive. Where the stakeholder would understand and be able to articulate the vision, it is the executive that defines the vision. It is the level at which the right data can influence company strategy. Certainly, not every dashboard will involve the executive, but a truly impactful one could rise to that level of awareness.

Of course, there is the rare situation where the executive could also be the stakeholder and the end user. If this is the case, then ensuring alignment is even more critical. More time needs to be spent on the desired outcomes as the dashboard can feed back directly and inform strategy in a virtuous loop.

The data owner

Someone is responsible for where the data is, how it is stored, how to get access to it, etc. It may be one person, possibly several, it could be a whole department. Whatever the case is, there is an individual who knows about the data. They have insight into the data sources, the data quality, the various issues with it, and more. This person might also be an end user, the BI developer, or play another role. The larger the organization, the more likely it is that the role is uniquely filled.

Naturally, there may be many people that have this knowledge about the data. There is the data that actually exists but consideration must also be given to data that does not exist but that might be needed. A degree of creativity is needed in this role in order to support the vision and needs of the business.

The data engineer

In some regards, this role can have overlap with the data owner. But where the data owner is a custodian, the data engineer is a builder. Their role is to architect and structure the data to serve it up in a way that the BI developer can easily access it. Why is this important?

Because this role is the glue between the business needs and the data reality. It is vital to have a value-focused mindset in this role. If that mindset is not there, then there must be a mechanism to be able to convey the value to this role in a transparent manner.

The BI developer

The BI developer is tasked with building the interface that the end users will interact with. In a typical software development project, the terms user interface (UI)/user experience (UX) are common. However, in BI, user experience is a rare expertise to be found in a BI developer. Yet we are trusting this role with the skills needed to develop, design, and engage the end user with a compelling user experience of the data.

With this burden of responsibility, this role needs as much context and background as possible on who the end user is and what their goals are for this project.

The data scientist

STORY

At the start of my analytics career, if I took an honest look at myself, I was not comfortable interacting with people. I'd actually go out of my way to not have to have a conversation with anyone I didn't know well. If you've worked in analytics for any length of time you would appreciate that there are quite a few introverts working in the field. It attracts a type of mind that is required to do analysis and explore fields and tables, come up with hypothesis, and experiment. It's a good thing.

One of my first analytics projects had me partnered with a group of PhD data scientists. I was the extreme extrovert in relation to them. They would ask me for tips on how to make presentations and how to elicit feedback in a constructive way. These folks were genuinely lost when it came to being successful in conveying the value of what they did to a group of people. This became painfully obvious when I was able to observe how they ran a data science project.

They had been tasked with producing a product that could predict the spread of probability you would need to buy real estate in a blind auction. The details are not important, but it was a brilliantly technical and intelligent approach they had taken to building the predictive model. There was only one problem. They had never spoken to the end users. There was exactly zero input from the people this product was going to be sold to.

It was the perfect storm. This team had to present their work to both the market, the potential buyers, as well as to their leadership. Consider the degree of discomfort. It was a meeting, other people were going to be there. Some of those people were the potential buyers that they did not properly understand. The rest were their peers, colleagues, and leadership.

Imagine the stress and tension being experienced by these data scientists. Of course, they knew they were going into a room to tell a bunch of subject matter experts how they should be thinking about their own industry. Without ever having spoken to them! I had made my case weeks earlier to this team. Talk to the experts! You must get their perspective. While I couldn't exactly put my finger on it, I believe there were two main reasons they did not. The first, because they would rather be building a predictive model than talk to people and, the second, they felt they were smarter than the experts. They had an advantage over the person who did not leverage data.

More on this story later.

The data scientist brings more advanced insight that goes beyond basic reporting. Not all projects will have the data scientist role. Not all projects need the sophistication provided by this role as many organizations struggle to even deliver on basic reporting.

However, for those that do have the data scientist role, it is one that will greatly benefit from being able to engage with the business. Better yet, have the data scientist be involved in the early stages of the journey to understand the motivations and interests of the end user.

The consultant

The consultant role is specifically called out here as this is the person who adheres to the principles in this book. They are the holder of the keys to value. They orchestrate the process throughout the journey and ensure value is in the center-stage.

It is an informal role, as very few organizations are structured this way. It could also be a bridge role. A bridge between the technical people and the non-technical businesspeople. The consultant attempts to maintain a third-party perspective, as if looking in from the outside, and helps steer the project down the right path.

The project manager

This is the role that orchestrates the steps along the project journey. They plan the work, break it down into smaller pieces, and assign that work to the respective roles. While a waterfall approach can work, the process in this book will be more effective with an agile format for project management execution. As such, this role breaks the work down into sprints via user stories over one- to two-week periods.

The business analyst

The business analyst role has some overlap with the consultant role. Their function is to understand and interpret what important information is available in the data and to appropriately shape that for the end users. This role ensures the project is delivering the "So what?" The role understands the vision of the stakeholders and executives. They help guide others along the path to achieve that vision.

In many organizations, this role might be blended with the BI developer role, as well as the consultant role. On the flip side, a larger-scale project may have several business analysts, especially where there are many end users and more effort is needed for change management, training, and enablement.

STORY

Continuing the data scientist story, everyone was in the room, ready for the big impact of what this new data science effort was going to have on the market. The energy was one of excitement but also cynicism. The doubt was coming from the industry experts. The team was ten minutes late. It took them a few more minutes to connect their laptop to the projector. After a few failed attempts, the presentation was ready to start.

The first few slides were all focused on the technology the team had used. It then got into how the model was built. They were about to get into a deep dive of the algorithms when one member of the audience, an industry expert, shouted "So what?! We don't care. What can it do? Why is it better than what we use now?"

This completely derailed the presentation. Some of the data science team were whispering to each other. Someone suggested moving on to the next slide. Another wanted to just ignore the person and carry on with the presentation. The lead data scientist stepped up.

He said "It is vastly superior to going by intuition and experience. There's no comparison." It simply wasn't a question, of course it was better. Experience counts for nothing when compared to using their predictive model. You could see the disdain on several of the audience's faces. Whether the statement was true or not, the lead data scientist was not winning the audience over.

It was a complete mess and a tremendous learning for me. With the benefit of hindsight, there was a consistent failure to communicate. A typical "people" problem. At an individual level, the people in the project team were not comfortable talking to the end users and stakeholders. They lacked the perspective from these roles, went off into their own bubble, and worked in isolation. It was almost impossible to be successful. However, it did give me insight into what a process would need in order to enable these people to be successful.

Release timeline

Aligning on expectations early and often reduces the friction of the entire process. One large, and often unrealistic, expectation is when a dashboard can be released. The sooner this is agreed the better, but not before the previous steps have been completed. Think of it like a sales process. The vision, the big picture, has been established. We have agreed on what the path is to get there and, finally, how we are going to travel down that path. It has placed the vision in our sights. Now it is time to discuss how realistic it is, and how fast we can travel down that path.

Now is the perfect time to start to address the reality of what kind of shape the data is in. Not a deep dive, that will come later, but a high-level appreciation that is both constructive and informative. A sort of thumb-in-the-air assessment. Since the outcomes and actions to be taken are already understood and agreed upon, it is easier to establish which data sources are needed.

For each data source, a scale of three is used to quickly rate across data that is missing, incomplete, does not exist, is unclean, if it is available, and other. It is important that this be high level. The objective is to inform and educate on what state the data is currently in so a discussion on timelines can be facilitated.

With a surface-level understanding of the data situation, a high-level timeline can be discussed. It can only be directional at this point. It is almost a certainty that the data is now going to be in perfect shape and some effort will be needed before all the desired outcomes can be properly measured by a dashboard. It is for this reason, among others, that an iterative release plan be implemented. The first version of the dashboard might be available relatively soon, but it will only facilitate aspects of the goals for which data is currently available. Subsequent iterations would have more time to work on the data and be able to expose more information on the dashboard.

Who and what will be impacted?

Change is part of delivering an impact. This is particularity true when there is tight alignment between business strategy and the dashboard visualizations. To maximize the potential for the impact of the dashboard and to mitigate some of the risk, attention must be given to who is going to be impacted by the change. Consider this a proactive way of reducing friction with people later in the project.

Identifying "change gaps" will help us to establish where focus may be needed. For example, consider a new dashboard that will have 1,000 users. This will put a requirement on the IT team to provide more support for that user population. Change is not just limited to people but also tools and processes. In this example, additional load is being placed on servers and more capacity is necessary, which increases costs. Which has an impact on the budget. It is preferable to have these conversations early, than in a reactive and higher-stress situation.

STORY

During a Q&A session about data strategy at a conference in Florida, an audience member was somewhat embarrassed to say that her organization had siloes. She thought that was abnormal, hence her reluctance to say it. But she was really struggling with it. Some commotion broke out in the audience with phrases being shouted out like "My company is a silo, within a silo, within a silo!", "You are not alone!", and "We have as many siloes as there are people!"

This last comment stuck with me. It might sound a little flippant, but it is the case. I used to look at siloes as something that needed to be solved. After some years of maturing and realizing that many smarter people than I have tried and failed, I eventually realized it is not something we can solve. However, bridges can be built between siloes. This subtle mental adjustment has large implications for increasing the adoption of analytics.

The strategy template

Everything covered in this chapter comes together in the strategy template. It is the first step in the journey and provides a valuable reference throughout the project and lifecycle of the dashboard. It provides context to people that become involved later in the effort, such as a BI developer, where they can look at the strategy and understand the context and desired outcomes. It provides a means of sharing and communicating the purpose. It is the anchor for all parties involved in creating the dashboard but also for the end users of the dashboard.

Before proceeding to the next chapter, you can download a digital version of the template from the book's website, as well as see case studies and examples of how to use it:

www.deliveringdataanalytics.com

03

UX principles

STORY

Early in my career I had an almost evangelical zeal about adhering to data visualization best practices. I felt I knew everything there was to know about designing the best-looking dashboards and it was a singular focus for me. I was about to get a rude awakening when data visualization best practices had a head-on collision with user experience principles. Up until that time, I would lean towards design versus experience.

Well, when working with a senior executive in a large automotive manufacturer, a dashboard I was working on challenged my perspectives and made me a far more effective consultant. The challenge was, one of the executive's direct reports was trying to give me some helpful advice as to what kind of charts his boss typically liked. Pie charts were the order of the day. Naturally, I scoffed and brushed him off as a sort of old school thinker. I was here to innovate and make the visualizations more intuitive and faster to act upon. Mostly, however, I wanted to impress with my ability to design pleasing user interfaces.

A week later, the dashboard was ready for prime time and end user testing. Probably some of my finest work. Not a pie chart in sight. The executive looked at it and then looked at me and said "Change those charts for pie charts or you are out." Pie charts were back on the menu! And, just like that, I learned that user experience beats data visualization best practices.

The seven principles of user experience

In Chapter 1, user experience was defined as the perceptions and responses a person has when interacting with a system, in this case a report or dashboard. When a user is interacting with data, the experience must be understood, designed for, and then measured. Is it a positive experience? What could be improved? How about load times and refresh rates?

In the field of user experience, there are generally seven factors that contribute to the experience. These were popularized by Peter Morville and have particular application to the end user's experience of data:

- useful
- usable
- findable
- credible
- desirable
- accessible
- valuable

Useful

Why would anyone adopt a dashboard that is not useful to them? If it does not have some benefit to using it, then it is improbable that it would become part of their workday. Indeed, they may have a spreadsheet that is more useful to them and a new dashboard would have to be significantly more valuable to overcome the inertia of switching technologies.

Whether or not something is useful is subject to interpretation and perspective, which must be considered. What a BI developer deems useful may not be so for the end user.

Usable

A usable dashboard is one that enables the end user to effectively and efficiently achieve the objectives the dashboard was designed for.

What it means is that the dashboard should become a tool for action and progressing work aligned to value. It should only have what is needed to fulfill this goal and no excess.

The temptation can be to have an array of bells and whistles like having as many filters as there are dimensions available in the source data. While it may seem effective, it may not be efficient, and hence will not be as usable. This is not to say it is all or nothing, there is certainly a gradient to usability, and it can improve through iterations as more user feedback is gathered.

Findable

Findable or discoverable means it must not only be easy to locate the dashboard in question but also it must be possible to answer the questions within the dashboard. It sounds obvious, but if the dashboard cannot be found then it will not be used and, hence, not adopted. If it is not adopted, then people will not be acting on the information in there and the whole purpose of the effort fails.

Many professionals miss this point. It comes down to a question of ownership and who is responsible for making a dashboard discoverable. While that owner is somewhat more obvious for the content within the dashboard, it is less so for the dashboard at large.

Credible

Credibility directly relates to trust, especially trust in the data being presented. As the adage goes, it takes time to build trust, but it can be lost in seconds and can be doubly hard to regain. When presented with a new experience, credibility with the end user must be a priority.

Consider the situation of a person using their spreadsheets. It may not be the best experience, but they trust it, it is credible to them. It is the credibility benchmark for their acceptance. Therefore, any new experience will be compared to it. If that new experience is not credible then they are likely to revert to their previous experience.

However, credibility is not just about trust in the data, it is also about the dashboard being fit for the intended purpose. The experience is credible for that specific end user. Should the user think the dashboard creator is trying to manipulate or deceive them then the relationship will be damaged.

Desirable

There are many tools and means to deliver insight. A spreadsheet is a very popular interface but contrast it to a beautifully designed, interactive, multi-device dashboard. If it did everything the spreadsheet accomplished but much more, it would have greater desirability.

Take the example of a regular plastic shopping bag and a Hermes handbag. They are both useful, usable, and findable but the Hermes is definitely more desirable. The plastic bag has a certain practical appeal, and it depends on usage; one probably would not carry shopping in a Hermes handbag. Nonetheless, the plastic bag is not desirable.

Desire is drawn from a composite of brand, identity, appearance, and emotional design. People tend to brag about items that are desirable. The more people talk about them, the more desirable they will become to a wider group of people.

Accessible

Accessibility in analytics and BI is both greatly misunderstood and underutilized. Accessibility relates to enabling a positive experience for the whole population through the spectrum of disabilities including impaired vision, hearing loss, motion impairment, and those with cognition challenges.

The challenge is that designing for accessibility is not at the forefront of the mind of the designer for several reasons, but two of the leading ones are a lack of awareness and the incorrect perception that there is not a critical enough mass of people with disabilities to make it worthwhile designing for. Whatever the justification, it is unacceptable. According to the CDC, one in four people in the United States have some form of disability. While not all of these have a disability that would affect a dashboard interaction, it is certainly a very large percentage that, if one wanted to make the argument, justifies making an accessible experience.

Perhaps a surprising outcome from designing for accessibility results in a more thoughtful and intuitive experience for all users, not just those with disabilities. In the modern era it is critical to design for accessibility. So much so that not doing so can cause risk expose to litigation. Indeed, there are legal practices that make a living from suing public-facing companies for not making their customer interactions accessible. Some companies mandate adherence to accessible standards to ensure awareness and proper implementation.

Valuable

Dashboards without value are legion. They are the norm in the enterprise. Low-value dashboards are easily created, little thought is needed to create them, and they are most easily produced in siloes. So, it is of little surprise that value is the key driver for the factors of a positive user experience.

Value can be interpreted on two levels: value for the end user, and value for the business. Ideally, both are true, but they are not always so and perhaps not always necessary. A dashboard can be valuable to the business but have little value to the end user. Conversely, a dashboard can have significant value to the end user but lack value to the business.

Without value in the equation, adoption will suffer. All the other aspects of a great user experience can be met and there may be fleeting adoption but, without value, the dashboard will fade into the background. To some, value can be the time-saving of automating four hours of manual data preparation into a dashboard that does the work automatically. To others, it might be being able to use data to identify customers with the highest potential of being cross-sold a new product. There are many paths to value. Regardless of which is chosen, value is the driving force.

The user experience formula

The good news is that by making an experience useful, usable, findable, credible, desirable, accessible, and valuable, there is a high probability that it will be adopted. Conversely, miss one of these and it may put the rest at risk. Imagine excelling at six of the factors but the data and experience is not credible. It is not trusted. Much of the effort and investment that went into the project might have been in vain. However, it also does not mean that all seven factors must be perfectly executed. Some will be more important than others, depending on the situation, who the users are, the context, and other aspects.

It can seem overwhelming for those without any exposure to user experience, but much of it is common sense and comes naturally already. Once there is awareness of the principles then it becomes easier to align with them. Oftentimes the challenge is just having the opportunity to address them; where in the fast pace of the workday does one find the time? While many people would agree that the principles make sense and should be applied, applying them is the blocker. Not only that, but who should be applying them?

STORY

I was guest speaking at a university about analytics adoption, talking to a group of aspiring data analysts. The topic was how to become a more effective data professional and how to hit the ground running when you start your analytics career. While going through the important aspects of user experience and who should own it, a hand was raised near the back of the auditorium. In general, I like to deal with questions as they come so I let the individual who had raised their hand ask their question:

"Nick, I have a simple question for you. Who should be doing all of this?"

"You!" was my reply.

Of course, I followed up with some more detail and explained that most organizations are not set up to have either the skills needed or the operating model to adhere to the UX principles. Therefore, no one else it going to do it and if you want your work to have an impact you must care about user experience.

Who owns user experience?

Many data professionals would greatly benefit from understanding some of the basic concepts from the field of user experience. Even adhering to some of the basic principles will have a significant impact on adoption. Indeed, several UX principles should take precedence over some of the typical activities that a data professional would engage in. Without adoption, for example, the time invested in the most beautifully designed dashboard would have been better spent in understanding what would be valuable to the end user. Maybe value for the end user is not a vibrant dashboard.

What this means is that by applying these UX principles there can be considerable time savings in addition to delivering high-adoption experiences. Everyone benefits from this, not least the person or team doing the work. For that reason, whoever is responsible for delivering the dashboard is the one that owns the user experience. A compelling user experience does not just happen by accident. It is carefully thought out and the result of a deliberate adherence to the seven principles.

User experience is an end-to-end responsibility and requires a holistic approach and process. One does not generally get lucky with it. If there is "luck" and adoption is high, it is potentially because there is no alternative experience or the experience it is replacing is so painful that any alternative is preferable. Applying UX methodologies ultimately makes the team more effective and their outputs more valuable, their end users driving more value and the stakeholders happier. It is a recipe for success.

At this point, the reader might be thinking that there is not the time in the day to become an expert in a new field. Fortunately, deep expertise in the UX field is not needed to realize some of the value; however, an understanding of the methodologies and approaches is necessary before diving into leveraging analytics and BI specific applications of UX.

Answering the why, what, and how

When donning the UX hat, the data professional must consider *why*, *what*, and *how* the data will be used. Understanding the end user motivations for adopting the dashboard will answer the *why*. What is the task it will help them complete and does it align to their goals and values? The functionality of the dashboard is considered the *what*. What can the end users do with the dashboard? The *how* is addressed by the design of the dashboard and its accessibility, desirability, and aesthetics.

As one might expect, it makes the most sense to start with understanding the *why*. This leads to designing the *what* followed by the *how* as the path to high-adoption dashboards.

UX disciplines

User experience is a tremendously vast term that encompasses a broad set of approaches. They can generally be bucketed into four disciplines: experience strategy (ExS), interaction design (IxD), information architecture (IA) and user research (UR). It is typical for a UX professional to only focus on one or two of these areas and to have a deep specialization. Without question, going deep on them is beneficial but probably impractical for many data professionals. For analytics purposes, a surface understanding of all areas is necessary.

Experience strategy (ExS)

Experience strategy deals with the alignment of the value chain from the needs of the end user to the goals of the stakeholder to the strategy of the business. The simpler this value chain is, the more likely it is to be surfaced and acted upon.

Interaction design (IxD)

Interaction design is the practice of determining how the end user should interact with a system, in this case the dashboard or report.

Any interactive elements must be considered from navigation tabs, filters, and drilldowns, to chart interactions. Focus is given to how intuitive the interaction is and how a user can quickly get to what they need.

Information architecture (IA)

Not to be confused with data architecture, information architecture is the organization of content within an interface so the user can easily access it. It should allow the user to achieve their goals in an efficient and user-friendly way. In the context of a dashboard, it can relate to the overall layout of KPIs, filters, charts, and navigation as well as the content within each of those areas.

User research (UR)

When a new product is being released to the market, extensive research can be done in understanding the problem it is solving, to inform the design of the solution. The intent being to understand and solve for the needs to the target audience as well as their behaviors, experiences, and motivations. This requires gathering inputs from the potential customers. These inputs can come in the form of interviews, surveys, and testing.

By understanding the end user in this way, it is easier to develop a sense of empathy and walk in their shoes. It forms the basis for user-centered design and will help others, such as BI developers and data engineers, to appreciate where the design is coming from. A typical challenge in design is bias. The designer has a preconceived notion of how a dashboard should be designed and what should be in it. UR helps to reduce that bias by learning the end user's perspective.

A key output of user research is the creation of user personas.

The user persona

A persona is a representation of a generic user whose goals and challenges are the same, or similar, to a wider group of users. They are often portrayed as fictional and not a specific person so as to avoid naming names and personalities.

One way to help understand a persona is by a person's job function or role in the company. For example, take a sales manager. The title already conveys some information about what they might care about—sales and managing the sales pipeline. All sales managers probably have similar goals. Those goals are likely a more operational version of the goals the sales associates might have. However, their goals would be less strategic than the regional sales director's. Goals are a great place to start for defining the personas.

Personas can change over time, especially during user research. During interviews, it may be discovered there is substantial nuance between the goals of various sales managers, for example. Perhaps their goals vary by region or by product. In which case, there may be a need to have separate personas for them. Of course, there is a point of diminishing returns here as too many personas can be burdensome and not yield as much benefit.

Perfection in personas is not needed initially, as the uplift of taking a user-centered approach where one did not already exist is already substantial. Later iterations can dive deeper into more distinct personas, if necessary. In general, more personas equal more dashboards that need to be created. In simple terms, each persona should be having their own dashboard experience, catering to their goals. When the personas are too general then one extreme is building a dashboard that caters for all goals, with little nuance of specific personas. In such cases, adoption is at risk because it can be a challenge to deliver the necessary value to certain subsets of personas that may exist. At the other extreme, it is possible to have a persona specific to every end user. While those users will be more likely to have a more positive user experience, there is greater overhead in administering and maintaining those dashboards. A happy medium is necessary and, in general, a good place to start is with existing corporate roles to define personas, and potentially define one subset of personas from there, if it appears that there are sufficient.

Breaking down the persona

In the field of UX, personas can have great depth and much detail. From understanding their interaction with existing systems, to recording and tracking their eye movements when using interfaces, a lot of effort can be spent here. However, for the purposes of analytics and BI, simplicity will be the order of the day.

A persona should address the following areas:

- background
- goals
- challenges
- preferences

Background

Imagine someone who was not involved in the user research will be looking at this persona, and needs to understand who this dashboard is for. The background will give them a surface appreciation of this. Items such as title, a role description, years of experience, etc. It is the detail someone might impart when introducing themselves in the context of their work. For example, "Hi, I'm Mary. I'm currently a director of marketing and I've been in marketing for the past ten years, mostly focused on building brand identity." Even that small amount of detail is helpful to someone who needs to design for Mary. More detail is certainly welcome, but a balance must be struck between more detail on the persona background and getting stuck into their goals.

Goals

Persona goals are where the rubber hits the road. The hope is that, following several interviews of the intended end users the persona is representing, common goals surface. The goals describe the motivations for the persona. They should be concise and easily understood. Extending the example of Mary's persona, her goals might be:

- Double brand awareness in the next two years.
- Increase positive customer sentiment towards the brand by 10 percent.
- Reach two million new customers through ad spend within the next year.

These examples of goals are all measurable, clear, and concise. They also serve to inform all parties involved in the project what is motivating this persona. In addition, they support selecting data that is aligned to achieving these goals.

Challenges

A challenge is typically a barrier or issue someone has in achieving a certain task or reaching their goals. There could be a great many, but a persona should surface the largest ones and those most related to the project at hand. For Mary's persona, her current challenges might look like:

- Data quality is very poor and not trusted.
- It takes extensive manual effort to bring data into a spreadsheet to do basic analysis.
- There is a lack of agreement on how to measure customer engagement.

It would be hoped that the project at hand could tackle some of these challenges either in full or part, perhaps by use case or some other subset. Solving any of these makes Mary happier and more of an advocate, but it is also important to know what barriers might exist that could prevent the success of the project.

Preferences

Every person has preferences. In the case of the persona, those preferences are related to the user experience. To design the future user experience, the current experience must be understood. Whether or not the persona likes the current experience is important, but it is also important to understand what they are familiar with. Parting with familiar interfaces brings its own risks. Therefore, the first step in improving the experience is understanding the base line. As an example, for Mary it might look like:

- Uses spreadsheets for all data-related activities.
- Usually uses a desktop but would like to see some data via her phone.
- A daily refresh of the data is desired—currently it is weekly.

Of particular importance is the data refresh, both the current and desired states. This can have a significant impact on assessing the data needs and informing the user experience of the dashboard.

Bringing it all together

The persona sets the foundation for everything to come, and care must be taken to get this right. Often, many reasons for poor adoption can be traced back to the persona stages. Poorly defined, or incorrect, personas can lead to issues down the road so this aspect must be taken seriously and only ever skipped if there is already deep familiarity with the end user.

Even in cases where the end user is unavailable one should still go through the persona exercise to "walk in their shoes." It can be a relatively useful activity and helpful for discussions with others about the approach. Regardless of the situation, leveraging templates for the persona will speed things up and are part of the adoption toolkit.

There are many persona templates available to suit various needs. Visit the book website for several examples and a reusable template in PowerPoint format for ease of editing and sharing.

Now that the foundation is set, the requirements need to be gathered for the persona(s).

04

Requirements gathering

As has often been the case in my analytics consulting career, a client would bring me in to help them solve their reporting and data adoption challenges. In one such instance, a large mining client needed some help. An important detail is that the people bringing me in usually represent the stakeholder or the executive role. It is rarely the end user role that is engaging my services and those of my firm.

My first meeting with the client was in one of the upper floors of a skyscraper they owned in its entirety. The meeting was about to get started. I assumed we were about to do introductions; however, one of the team stood up and said "My safety story I want to share today comes from this past weekend when I was packing my kids into the car." He proceeded to relate how taking an extra five seconds to check the car seat restraints for kinks or twists would greatly reduce the risk of the child seating failing to successfully protect his children.

Everyone in the room had their turn to share a safety related experience they had recently learned from. While I was still catching up as to what was going on, it was my turn. Fortunately, it was a well-attended meeting and I had time to think of a good safety story I could share. I felt I had a rich pool of safety stories I could pull from, having grown up in Ireland with several friends who lived on farms.

The instance I shared was when one of my friends, Martin, had managed to build a cannon that would shoot frozen oranges. This was obviously very dangerous and clearly presented a safety risk to both people and the farm animals. Martin wouldn't have been known as a safety officer, that was certain. I expressed that this was an example of a poor level of safety and how Martin's parents shouldn't have allowed him to build frozen orange cannons.

Well, that wasn't the right answer. All the folks in the room looked disapprovingly at me. I felt uncomfortable. Storytelling, I felt, was one of my strong suits. However, as has often been the case in my career, the storytelling wasn't the problem. As I was about to find out, the problem was my inaction in that story.

One of the meeting participants took the time to explain the problem with my story. "This is an example of a failure to take control of a volatile situation. You demonstrated how many unsafe situations can spiral to have dangerous or lethal consequences. You did nothing, worse yet, you blamed people who were not even there. You acted like you were just along for the ride, like you had no agency in safety. What could you have done to make it a good safety story?"

Ah, now I got it. The idea was not to share dangerous situations but to share situations where I took the time to improve safety. I said I should have handcuffed Martin to the house as soon as I had arrived at his place. Having Martin in shackles would probably be the best outcome we could hope for in terms of safety. While not the perfect answer, the objective of this practice stuck with me.

It was absolutely second nature for this organization to start a meeting in this way. It was embedded into the culture of the organization. Every single meeting was started this way. I was to find out later that this massive mining organization had gone from having tens of deaths per year down to zero. This practice was literally life or death for them. It was why they took it so seriously. This one action transformed the safety culture of the whole organization. An absolute intolerance for unsafe practices and a proactive mindset towards safety. It was seeded from the top of the organization and made its way down to every single meeting at all levels.

This was my first experience of a wholesale cultural shift. It was possible. A massive, global firm, with tens of thousands of employees could affect such impact.

Could something similar be done with data?

One of the highest impact activities that organizations fail to do effectively is communicating. In the business intelligence and analytics world, that failure is even more significant. It is a challenge that, if left to its own devices, will produce a massive pile of dusty reports and dashboards that stagnate and cost an organization time, money, and resources. It must stop.

A cultural shift in data mindset is necessary. Leveraging data in every conversation so it becomes a commonplace part of making plans and decisions. There are several ways of achieving this. The most comprehensive is to have a top-down initiative, coming from the C-suite, that has consistent messaging about becoming a data-driven organization. Naturally, it takes time for such a shift to happen and become instilled in all the employees.

The bottom-up approach

The term "storytelling" is frequently used in relation to how dashboards should be designed. It advocates having a compelling story, or narrative, within a dashboard to make it relevant and captivating to the end user and to drive some action or outcome. It is an important and necessary practice. However, there is a more impactful and vital story to be told. It is the story of adoption. It is the story of how people can be taken on the journey to use data as part of their planning and decision process. By looking at this like a story, with many chapters, it can give the more realistic mindset that change takes time. It will not be achieved by one dashboard alone. This is the bottom-up strategy.

It entails taking a specific department, use case, or scenario and applying some basic processes. An effective way of tackling this is through a dashboard. Since a dashboard should be focused on specific outcomes it is trying to achieve, it will already have a defined set of users and a business case it is addressing. The dashboard becomes an ideal mechanism to attach the "bite sized" cultural shift, one dashboard at a time.

Over time, more and more people are touched by the process and become more comfortable with it. Small victories are achieved along the way and social proof builds a wave of momentum that there is a new and effective way to get access to data and make one's job easier.

Indeed, it helps people become outstanding and can accelerate their career.

The key to starting the bottom-up approach lies in the realm of user experience (UX). Specifically, user research. User research is what it sounds like, a means of better understanding the end users. It can include interviews, workshops, persona development, and other methodologies.

The two types of interviews

User research is difficult to reliably perform without some interaction with the intended target audience. It can take many forms, but is most often conducted in person or via video chat. There are two distinct types of individual that need to be interviewed, the stakeholders and the end users. The stakeholders may have already been engaged in the strategy stage, but if they have not or there are other stakeholders that were not included to date it is the ideal time to elicit input from them.

By the end of the interviews there will be two sets of goals documented: one from the stakeholders and one from the end users. It will quickly become apparent whether these goals are aligned or not. Do the end user goals roll up to the goals of the stakeholders? Are the goals mismatched? Are the stakeholder goals too tactical? Answering these questions and, most importantly, flagging them is vital. Some misalignments can be tackled over time, through iterations. Others might be intractable, and no number of dashboards will help.

STORY

A typical reaction from stakeholders can be that there is no need to interview the end users of a report or dashboard. Depending on the situation, I will usually push back on that. In one such situation, I was working with a client that had strong feelings about how the dashboard should look and who said that I did not need to engage with the end users because "they don't know what they really want." While that might have been true, there is almost always value to be gained in unexpected ways.

After some discussion, we agreed that I could conduct a few interviews, almost under protest. I did not need more than five minutes per interview to see a common issue that was a complete deal-breaker for building a new dashboard. All the users answered in the same way to one of my first interview questions: "How do you currently access your reports and dashboards?"

The consistent answer was: "I don't."

The end users already had some dashboards, not perfectly executed but there was certainly value in them. The challenge was that the end users either didn't know where to find them or the links they had to them didn't work.

The problem was not going to be solved by building new dashboards, it was a delivery problem. Of course, this was news to the stakeholder, and we pivoted the project to focus on enabling discovery of existing dashboards instead of building a new one.

Answering questions

With the wide range of people involved in BI and analytics projects, there is a broad span of technical understanding, from those with deep technical experience to those with little to no technical expertise. While businesspeople might have deep domain or industry knowledge, it is often not married with skills in data preparation and data visualization. The same goes for the data scientist who could write R scripts in their sleep but would not know the difference between gross and net margin.

What it all means is that people can very easily get lost along the way. They may not feel comfortable trying to articulate their domain knowledge perspective in technical terms or vice versa. A data engineer may struggle to speak the language of a subject matter expert in contract pricing. A simple common standard is needed. Simple being the key term here. The answer? Natural language. The common vernacular we use day in and day out to query reality. Specifically, using natural language questions as the basis for all future discussions around the data and the dashboard. Of course, there are good and bad ways of framing a question to be easily understood. A question like "How are our sales doing?" has a great many ways to be misinterpreted. However, reframing it like this has specificity and is easy to understand: "What is our gross sales revenue so far this year?" It is both clear and concise, yet a BI developer can easily interpret the intent of the question and start to navigate the data for the fields to consider including. Stakeholders and end users alike can have a shared understanding of the questions.

The questions become the fabric of the dashboard journey. They are woven into the requirements gathering, are used for selecting data and informing the data model, become the title of charts in the dashboard, and the basis for training materials and supporting adoption.

Making questions the basis for a successful dashboard and, ultimately, the adoption of data-driven decision-making, has several key benefits. BI and analytics can be perceived as overly technical. A little like a black box, hidden behind a shroud of complexity. Using questions can help reduce the friction for people to get involved and to understand what the dashboard is about. Simply by reading the questions it is going to answer, assuming the questions are well-formulated, the reader can quickly appreciate the context and value.

In addition, new users are quickly brought up to speed. People do not have the time to consume detailed training materials. Indeed, the modern interfaces of today must be intuitive and easy to understand, even if the underlying system is complex. Complexity must be abstracted from the user. As a result, questions reduce the need for extensive documentation.

With increased simplicity comes the possibility to engage inputs from a wider range of people. People who can now understand the context and no longer be bystanders. They can have agency in the process, be part of the requirements journey, and see how it progresses throughout the dashboard lifecycle.

Finally, and possibly most importantly, significant time can be saved. Stakeholders and end users can become aligned much earlier in the process. Rather than waiting to give a reaction until the dashboard is built, they can get a reasonable sense of what value it will have just by reading the questions it will be answering. This would happen much earlier in the process. The developer saves time on reducing the amount of rework that is needed. The data engineer can be more targeted in what the data model needs to look like.

For those reasons, special care must be taken in the formulation of questions.

Formulating a question

For a question to be effective, it must meet several criteria. It must be:

- in natural language
- in the form of a question
- easily understandable for the end user persona
- not too high level
- granular enough to be discreetly answered by data
- possibly bucketed by time

What this means is that a question can be simple enough to be easily understood but also have enough fidelity of detail to be used to make a first pass at what data will be needed to answer it. This balance must be struck. It is not a simple prospect but taking this effort here, early on, pays large benefits later in the development stages.

Sometimes it is easier to see some bad examples, to observe what not to do. Here are examples of poorly formed questions:

- Are we doing well?
- What are our sales?
- How is our supply chain doing?
- Are we winning?
- Should we change our strategy?

Sure, we can make sense of what those questions mean, but they are unhelpful to the person who needs to go and create the visualizations to answer them and, more challenging yet, for the person who needs to build the data model. These are the types of questions that a stakeholder or executive would be asking, and they may even contain an appropriate level of detail. However, they do not work for selecting data. To do that, adherence to the questions criteria is needed. The following are examples of well-formed questions:

- What are our net revenue sales for last month?
- How many products have we shipped so far this year?
- Are we on track to hit our current financial year revenue goals?
- How many suppliers do we have?
- How fast does our inventory turn?
- How many customers made purchases so far this month?

Imagine being tasked with scouring through the data sources to try to answer these questions. It is much easier than with the previous set. This set of questions is clearer, with an appropriate level of detail. The first question cites "net revenue sales" as opposed to just "sales," which is open to interpretation and could have referred to the quantity of products sold, gross sales revenue, etc.

If more detail is needed, then it should be added to the question itself. If the reader must ask an additional question, such as "Is that net sales after or before tax?", then it needs to be specified in the question itself. A long question is preferable to a question that is not easily understood. Better to have someone comment on the specificity of a question rather than complain about the vagueness of it.

To differentiate, and emphasize their importance, these questions will be referred to as business value questions, or BVQs for short. The term is important because every BVQ should be aligned to value. It should have some path back to the goals and outcomes from the dashboard goals and strategy. This alignment must be made clear when determining the BVQs. There are several means to extract the BVQs; the primary approach is to conduct interviews.

Interview approach

While there is little novel about interviews in general, they are greatly underleveraged in BI and analytics. In part, it may be due to the types of personalities attracted to the field and their desire to minimize human interaction. Regardless, the value of interviews is immense, and a path must be found to facilitate them.

As one would expect, an interview involves the interviewer and the interviewee. It can be helpful to have someone take notes so the interviewer can focus on reading the body language and facial expressions of the interviewee. An interview typically involves the interviewer asking a structured set of predefined questions in such a manner that elicits the depth of response that is needed but is not adversarial or perceived as judgmental. Therefore, care must be taken. The risks must be considered.

Consider a scenario where an inexperienced data engineer, with few people skills and poor communication, is interviewing a senior executive. An executive who has been frustrated by the lack of insight and reporting coming from the team that the interviewer is a part of. This interview is likely to be a train wreck and is inadvisable as, rather than improve the outcomes, it could do damage and further erode trust and relationships.

Hear these words of caution and warning. Carefully assess who is conducting the interview and balance that with the seniority of and current relationship to the interviewee. For example, having a junior data analyst interview a senior executive might work, depending on the personalities involved, but it probably will not be as effective as it could be if they were closer in level. Another such example would be personality types. There are a great many personality type frameworks, some with upwards of 15 or 20 categories. While there is certainly value in having such a tremendous level of detail, there usually is just not the time. Too much complexity can make it difficult to execute and a balance must be reached between optimal process and actual execution of the process. It could indeed be argued that an incredibly impactful process, with great depth and nuance, has little value if it is not easily executed. For that reason, simplicity shall remain a priority.

In that light, let us consider two main personality types that should be considered, introverted and extroverted. Of course, there is far more to people that these vague definitions, but they are sufficient to guide some of the interactions. For example, the preference would be to match the personality type of the interviewee. Should the interviewer be introverted and the interviewee is extroverted, it would be advantageous for the interviewer to assert themselves a little more in the interview to better match the personality of the interviewee.

In cases where confidence is lacking, or of inexperience, prudence must be shown in minimizing the risk when interviewing an extroverted candidate. It is common sense but is often missed in the fast pace of the business environment. An ineloquent and stumbling interviewer is likely to frustrate and infuriate an executive.

There is most definitely an art to conducting interviews, but preparation can ease the nerves and even give a basis to form a good start to the interview. For some people, social interaction comes naturally. They have an innate comfort in talking to others and creating an atmosphere of openness. For others, for whom this does not come so easily, some background research into the interviewee can help. Without fail, LinkedIn is a rich resource for understanding the professional story your interviewee has been on, assuming they have a profile, of course. Where did they attend school? Did they move jobs a lot? Do they comment on specific posts and topics frequently? Is there anything to be gleaned that can give you an insight into their goals and passions? If there is, this could be a topic for an opening ice breaker in the interview.

STORY

One of my first ever analytics interviews that I conducted was with a C-suite executive of a global bank. While I feel like I am reasonably affable in person and can use humor to get people to relax, this interview was to be performed via a phone call, with no video. I didn't have much to go on but I knew he loved cricket. After my fifth visit to the bathroom, it was time to make the call at the scheduled time.

My main concern was that I would come across wooden and like I was reading from a script, which I was. So, I decided to chill out a bit at the start of the call and, when the interviewee picked up and we exchanged pleasantries, I asked how his week was going so far and how his favorite cricket team was doing. He enthusiastically started telling me how great the team was performing. For a solid ten minutes we had a heated discussion about cricket and the data and sites he would reference when trying to predict his team's performance. He ended by saying he wished his own company data was as easy to work with. How it was not trustworthy and the reports he received from his team were not aligned to his own calculations in Excel. I ended up dropping my script. I did not need it. I was having a very human and relatable conversation with someone who clearly cared about his company and how he could use data to make a difference, but he had barriers. This was exactly what I needed to hear.

Basically, there was no way the needle was going to move for his subordinates unless we found a way for this executive to trust the data his team was working on. This candid conversation shifted the underlying effort from reporting and dashboard development to data accuracy and quality and establishing transparent metric definitions. A script could have delivered me to the same destination, but it would have taken longer and been a lot less engaging.

Stakeholder interviews

The stakeholder holds the keys to adoption, business value, and the "So what?" The stakeholder(s) may have already been engaged at the strategy stage. If not, and this is the first time engaging with the stakeholders, it will be a great opportunity to refine the strategy template.

Conducting an interview can be intimidating. Especially so when that person is more senior than the interviewer. There are some helpful pointers to keep in mind. First, many people appreciate being asked for their opinion and being a participant in a process that is ultimately going to help them. So, it is better to see it as a partnership and entering the interview with that mindset will quickly become apparent to the interviewee. The last thing a stakeholder wants to hear is a know-it-all telling them how to operate their business or what they should be thinking about. The virtuous path is one of listening, empathy, and pointed probing. The skilled interviewer is like a samurai that does not waste blows on the armor of the opponent but executes precise cuts at the gaps in the armor. The dance is necessary in order to get to the core of transformation. It may be but a few words at the end of the interview, or the tone of the discussion, but one must be listening for it.

Finding time on the calendar of a stakeholder can be difficult. A common issue is not being able to get any time at all. The temptation is to bypass the interview, but one must persevere. While having an hour for the interview is the ideal amount of time, even just securing 15 minutes is far preferable to no time at all. There is a larger element at play than just the interview itself. It is the perception of engagement and opportunity for stakeholders to have a voice. If they do not have the time, they know they had the opportunity. As stakeholders are often senior and hold some sway in the organization, even if they are unable to attend an interview, visible effort must be made to accommodate them. It will pay dividends later.

When planning for a stakeholder interview, there are several important and desirable outcomes. First, the "So what?" needs to be understood from the perspective of this stakeholder. What is the impact this dashboard will have if properly implemented? It is a discussion of outcomes and a strategic way to set up the conversation. The interviewer should have a perspective on this before going into the interview.

It can open in several ways. Often the ideal way is to start with introductions and level-setting. Explaining to the stakeholder how the project started, some of the players involved, and the ultimate vision for the dashboard. This is followed with the context for why the interview is happening. It is part of a process to ensure all the important perspectives are collected and appropriately represented in the dashboard. To that end, a series of interviews are being conducted with the stakeholders to better understand how the dashboard can be successful, any potential barriers to that success, and what the stakeholders would like to see on the dashboard.

However, in the experience of the author, an element of icebreaking may be needed to build rapport at the start of the interview. This is where some of the background knowledge of the interviewee can be useful. There is almost always something to latch on to. It can be as obvious as referencing how their state or national team did in a recent game or perhaps the topic of a recent post they "liked" on social media. The first few minutes of the conversation establish a foundation. Upon this foundation the interviewer can build trust and relatability. It can relax the interviewee and let them feel they are going to be listened to, their perspectives valued.

Confidence comes with experience, but until then, having a set of prescribed questions, appropriately delivered, can be a sufficient replacement. At a minimum, a list of questions can help to frame a good conversation and keep the discussion on track. Over time, these questions will be asked differently, or may not be even asked at all. It is the answers the questions are trying to extrapolate that are most important, no matter how they are arrived upon.

With the introductions covered and some initial conversation, the core of the discussion can start. The following questions do not need to be followed exactly but the sentiment behind them and the order in which they are listed have proven to be beneficial. The first two questions are intended to get to the "So what?" and are more strategic in nature.

Stakeholder question 1: What is the motivation for having this dashboard?

It is a deliberately broad question designed to cast a wide net for responses from the interviewee. The conversation is still getting warmed up at this point, so specificity is not as important as simply gaining alignment on the topic and overall vision for the dashboard. It is ok if the answer is broad at this point. Attention must be paid to any friction the question might cause—forcing a tight focus at an early stage could unnecessarily jeopardize the interview.

Expect answers to be along the lines of having a single source of the truth, to defining common definitions for metrics for the given topic, and everything in between. This should not take long, and if any control were to be exerted by the interviewer at this point it would be to contain this question, to not occupy too much time.

Stakeholder question 2: What are the business value and outcomes you want to see from this effort?

Having spoken in general terms with the last question, the intent of this question is to determine the measurable value the dashboard should have. The stakeholder should be directed, if necessary, with some examples of specific outcomes for similar efforts. For example, the interviewer might list examples such as increasing sales by 5 percent, improving the customer net promoter score by three points, or lowering the cost of attrition by $25,000.

Chances are, the stakeholder will not be thinking a dashboard can do this, or maybe there are simply no strategic goals defined by the business. It may take some time to arrive at the outcomes. A little easier, perhaps, is to discuss in terms of business value that could be derived from the dashboard. If it is not possible to elicit measurable outcomes in the available time, then talking in broader business value concepts is a fallback position.

Stakeholder question 3: What are your current challenges in relation to reporting?

On occasion, it makes sense to start the interview with this question as it can clear the air and allow the stakeholder to be heard. It can also be an effective icebreaker. However, it can detract from the goals and take up a significant portion of the interview if not properly managed. For the inexperienced interviewer, this is the right sequence to ask this question. Challenges do not have to be directly in relation to the dashboard being discussed, as it is possible there are broader challenges that the interviewer needs to be aware of.

Again, it will be necessary to exert some degree of structure to this portion of the interview. It can be valuable, but it can also become a ranting opportunity with little value. In a rare circumstance, it may be exactly what is needed and a list of grievances might be the only thing to come out of the interview. Typical challenges might include not being able to find the data they need, when they want it, or the numbers being presented are simply wrong.

Stakeholder question 4: Has anything prevented this project from happening in the past?

This question is an important baselining opportunity. The stakeholder may have observed past attempts to tackle this same effort. Why did it fail in the past? Why would it succeed this time around? Is there anything novel to this iteration that would truly make it succeed or is it just the latest attempt at wishful thinking? Is it even worth attempting again?

Naturally, the answer may just be "No." In which case this question has served its purpose. However, if it has been attempted in the past then what were the key learnings and how, by understanding the past, can it succeed this time around?

Stakeholder question 5: What metrics do you currently look at?

A reminder that the stakeholder is not the end user of the dashboard. There must be a clear distinction between the two. However, the stakeholder may have a perspective that should at least be considered. The purpose of this question is to understand whether data is presently something they utilize and, if they do, what specific metrics they look at. This is ideally in relation to the project at hand. There is no need to spend much time here.

Stakeholder question 6: What metrics would you like to see?

The stakeholder may have some thoughts to share on what they think should be considered for the end user. It is not the final say, but their answer here will be compared to what the end user comes back with when interviewed later. In an ideal world, there will be alignment between the two. The answers from the stakeholder may be higher level and that is fine.

Stakeholder question 7: What are the top business value questions (BVQs) that you want answered from the data?

The final question may seem similar in objective to the prior one. It is a different way of asking the same thing but presenting it differently.

Sometimes, just using natural language to frame the need will yield different outcomes. Perhaps they struggled with the last question and came up with nothing. Their BVQs will likely be broad as this is the stakeholder and not the end user.

Expect to be leaving the interview with several BVQs that the stakeholder thinks are important to be able to answer for the end user.

A practical means of tracking the answers can be in PowerPoint with a simple template. Visit the book website to download one.

End user interviews

While similar in format to the stakeholder interviews, the end user interviews should be more tactical and have more focused outcomes. Specifically, these interviews are going to be the primary source for the BVQs.

End user interviews typically require more time due to the emphasis on defining a set of BVQs that the end user would like to have answered. However, it is still important to better understand them, their role, and objectives. For that reason, some of the questions are going to be similar to the stakeholder questions.

This is the end user, it is who is being designed for. What do they need to see in order to support their decision-making that aligns with the goals of the stakeholders?

End user question 1: What does your typical week look like?

This question is intended to be an icebreaker but also has the potential to better understand the end user and their role. Consider someone on the team who might be reading these notes later and does not have the opportunity to directly talk to the end user. What information would help them to understand their background and where they are coming from? This is often a gap that can exist for a BI developer or engineer that is far removed from the end user interaction and lacks context. The answer to this question can humanize who they are developing the dashboard for and enable them to "walk in their shoes."

Typical answers to this question range from considerable time being spent manually working with data to not even knowing where to find what they need. It is important to listen for any frustrations or stress. Do they talk in a negative or positive light? Tone is important to pick up on here. It can be freeform and meander a little, but the interviewer will need to hone it for the next questions.

End user question 2: How do you currently access and use data?

Where the last question was broad and open-ended, this question is narrow in focus and directly tied to how the end user currently leverages data in their role. The answer will help identify the level of sophistication and technical depth of the interviewee. Maybe they do not use data in their role at all, perhaps they do not know how. It could be that they are a power user and want direct access to a data catalog. There is a wide spectrum here, but the typical answer will be somewhere in between.

End user question 3: What are your current challenges in relation to reporting?

As the interview continues, ideally some rapport has been developed and the end user is comfortable sharing some of the challenges they have faced regarding how they leverage data in their role. The opportunity here is to identify any possible benefits and challenges that can be overcome with the new solution. Items to look for are time savings, manual effort, accessing multiple reports, etc.

This question can easily spin out of control into a griping session, so it is the role of the interviewer to contain the challenges to the current project and to wrap it up once the main points have been covered.

End user question 4: What goals do you have in your role and how can data help?

For some, this may be the first time they have been asked to identify what goals they have in their job. It is entirely possible they do not have anything specific. If this is the case, they will need a little time to think it through. It is important because their goals should align with the stakeholder goals, to a degree. Their goals should also align with the goals of the dashboard. As the end user, they are the instrument for the change that will come from the insights being made available. If they are not aligned, then that change is unlikely to happen.

The reality is that there will be some degree of misalignment between the various goals and that is ok. If there are significant misalignments, then they should be noted and the stakeholders should be made aware.

End user question 5: What metrics do you currently look at?

Similar to the question asked of the stakeholder, it baselines what they are used to seeing and, potentially, what they might expect to see in the new dashboard. In addition, it may be necessary to include some of these metrics, even if not directly applicable. The desire would be to avoid comments like "In my old report I was able to see X, Y, and Z. This new dashboard doesn't even have what I usually look at."

Change is incremental, not all at once, and people need to be brought on a journey. Do not worry if the current metrics do not align with the goals for the current effort; adoption is the aim of the game.

End user question 6: What metrics would you like to see?

More attention should be paid to the response to this question as it shows how the end user is framing what they think is important to them. The answers may lean more towards what they currently look at or may lack alignment to the goals and end vision. It is an intentional journey that is setting up the conversation for the next question where closer alignment can be revealed.

End user question 7: What are the top BVQs that you want answered from the data?

This is the natural language approach both to extracting what the user wants and also making alignment to goals more intuitive. These form the basis for the BVQs that will be leveraged throughout the process.

The exact framing of this question is important. "Business value questions" implicitly requires the interviewee to consider the value of any question and it empowers the interviewer to probe a little more and push back on questions that do not have business value. By the end of this interview there should be a list of BVQs. They should not be constrained by what data is available but be a "blue sky" list of what would be ideally answered for the end user.

Alternatives to interviews

Interviews are a compelling way to gather requirements. However, they are not the only way. Often, there is not the time to conduct interviews, or it may be more beneficial to have a group of people together to determine the requirements. In such cases a workshop may be preferable. On other occasions, there is benefit in conducting both interviews and a workshop. However, the workshop is not for the inexperienced and can add risk and potential increased friction that would not otherwise surface by conducting interviews alone.

0 5

Data assessment

It was early spring and one of my first opportunities in my analytics career to work with senior stakeholders. I was excited but also somewhat naïve in knowing what to expect. The project was to build a basic revenue dashboard that would surface all the important aspects of how the business was performing across all the various product lines. The senior stakeholders involved were each an owner of one of the product lines. They had strong opinions on what they needed to see and how they needed to see it.

In my very first workshop with them, I just went along with what they wanted, documenting all the business questions and any other questions that maybe didn't have any apparent value. Regardless, I wasn't about to push back and upset the apple cart. Who was I to question the business judgment of a group of senior executives anyway, and why should they take me seriously?

What resulted was a very wide range of questions they wanted a dashboard to answer for them. Many of these questions were not consistent across product lines. However, worse yet, most of the questions were not readily addressed by the available data. Several of them simply assumed that if they could imagine up a question it would be possible to answer it with data.

Instead of addressing that disconnect early in the process, and dealing with the resultant friction it would generate, I pushed it off. Perhaps I hoped they would just forget what they wanted. Well, three months passed, and the dashboard was ready and I had prepared a little demonstration of it for the executives in an hour-long presentation that was to also serve as training on the dashboard.

It did not go well at all. About five minutes in, someone said "Where's the rest of it?" Another individual highlighted, "This is much smaller in scale than I had expected!" I tried to talk about data quality and not being able to join several of the data sources, but I had dropped the ball—it was too late to work on alignment. The time to raise those issues was much earlier. The damage had been done and it was going to be a challenge to win back their trust.

By some margin, the most significant reason I am engaged by a client is to address the inability of their team to adequately understand the needs of the business. They either do not have the right process in place or they lack the seniority and leadership to drive requirements in a way that gives their business stakeholders agency in the process while also providing adequate push back. That push back is typically in the form of managing expectations of what is and is not possible with the available data.

On one extreme, from the perspective of the end user or the stakeholder, they might be told "No" a lot by their IT, BI, or analytics counterparts. Perhaps they need a report and want it fast, so a request is made to have it by the end of the week. The BI developer has a long backlog of requests they need to get through, so why should this one be put before others? In addition, maybe the data is just not available to build it quickly. In this setting, it appears reasonable for the BI developer to just say no. However, the requestor might perceive this negatively and does not have the context as to why the developer said no. In summary, there is little partnership.

In such an atmosphere, the requestor is less likely to trust the reasoning given for why something cannot be built right away. A common reason given is that of the state of the available data. While it can be a perfectly valid reason, it does not give much back in terms of a path forward. The requestor perceives it as an excuse or just another case where IT is being slow and inefficient. Naturally, over time, this calcifies into a barrier and erodes trust to the point where both parties find it futile to work together.

A path forward

In the prior chapter, the concept of BVQs was introduced to align the various parties on value and to take a strategic and "blue sky" view of what outcomes were desired from a dashboard. Producing those BVQs was an early step in partnership between the involved parties. A step that is either taken by one party alone or not done at all. It is more than simply partnership; it is a means of avoiding the "No."

The journey started with "Yes, let's make this work and start somewhere." That somewhere was the listing out of all the questions that would be valuable, irrespective of what shape the data is in. It is a pure exercise in identifying the value that could be realized if there were no bounds on the available data. The exercise is vitally important. Starting the journey with positivity over starting it with a data-led approach. The data-led approach would likely be more constrictive as it would only explore scenarios for which there is existing data. It can restrict creativity and growth to the small realm of what is possible given the current state.

In contrast, starting with less regard for the current state of data allows for broader thinking about what the business needs and can be used to set the roadmap for what data will be needed in the future and how to get it in order to achieve the desired vision. While there are merits to taking both approaches, building trust and adoption are best served by taking the visionary approach. This is partly due to starting in terms that businesspeople can directly relate to, business questions, and not the technical limitations of the available data.

In addition, starting this way also serves as a means to gain some degree of alignment on the intricacies of data and some of the related challenges. The journey is started on the right foot down a path that all participants can take. However, at some point the piper must be paid! At some point there must be the conversation of dealing with what the data reality is and it can only be delayed so much before that delay starts to cause its own problems.

STORY

While working with a large group of stakeholders, with varying degrees of technical understanding, I decided I would try out a scoring technique to see if it could be used as an opportunity to educate them on the challenges of data quality and availability to establish a baseline of understanding amongst the team.

During a workshop, we had a list of the questions all the folks wanted to be able to answer with a dashboard. I had asked one of the data engineers on the team to rank those questions by what he thought was feasible based on what he knew about the data. It was during the lunch break, so he had an hour to do this with his laptop and he executed some SQL queries to probe the various fields.

After the hour, the questions were ranked on a scale of 1 to 10. The rank of 10, placed at the top of the scale, meant that the data was readily available and easily accessible. Conversely, the rank of 1, at the bottom of the scale, basically had the meaning that the data did not exist at all. There were only a few questions near the top, most were in the 3 to 5 range, and several were at the 0 mark.

When the participants came back into the room, I related the purpose of the scale to them, and some heated discussion ensued. While I had only allotted 15 minutes for this activity, it took the best part of an hour to become aligned. Much of the debate was around why a certain question had such a low rank and the data engineer was able to illustrate why by directly showing the data to the participants and the lack of trust he had in the numbers, without some work being performed. Some of the questions were moved around a little and some were rephrased.

The initial intention of this activity was to educate, but there were several other benefits beyond that. We were able to pick an initial set of questions that could be reasonably addressed in a short period of time with a little bit of effort. This set of questions would inform the first iteration of the dashboard. More importantly, it appeared that this group appreciated that it would take time and they understood the rationale behind it. With the right investment and time, their questions would all be able to have answers.

Given the significant impact the activity had, from that point on, I formalized this method into a standard activity and made several refinements to it over the years.

Scoring business value questions

There are several ways to approach scoring a BVQ and several perspectives need to be considered. The journey of change management is the journey of shared agency and responsibility. This entails ensuring the necessary parties have a stake in the scoring. To achieve that, the scoring needs to be able to accommodate several dimensions where each dimension is addressing a different perspective. So, it is not simply a case of scoring based on the available data, it must be broader than that.

Deriving the dimensions of scoring must come from the roles already identified. For the stakeholder that might be cost and value. For the end user the dimensions are value and, to a degree, data quality. For the data owner the primary dimension is data quality and availability. Finally, for the BI developer and data engineer it is effort. There is certainly going to be overlap in who cares about what, but we can generally score a BVQ across these four dimensions:

- value
- cost effectiveness
- ease of effort
- data

This set of dimensions requires consensus and likely a degree of friction to get to that consensus. But consider the importance of arriving at this consensus. Every participant has a chance to have their voice heard and their perspective has a vehicle to be shared. It also affords each participant the opportunity to hear other perspectives and, over time, gain a greater appreciation of what it takes to succeed as well as deeper understanding into the challenges that their colleagues face. Its importance cannot be overstated.

With a set of dimensions established that can be used to score a BVQ, an appropriate scale is needed with which to score them.

The scoring scale

One of the scales that has become very familiar is the 5-point scale that is often found when online shopping. When buying a product, a shopper considers how close to a 5-star rating it has and that rating informs their purchasing decision to a significant degree. However, it is certainly not the only scale out there. Other common scales are the 3-point scale and the 10-point scale. There is also the "thumbs up/thumbs down" rating system in regular use. Of course, the popularity of those is applicable for reviews and product ratings but some of the merits carry over to use as a scoring scale for our purposes.

The first major consideration for the scale is the number of discrete intervals it should have. Starting at 2 and going up to 100 are typical. The lower range possibly lacks nuance and the upper range lends itself to potential needless disagreement, for example about whether a rating should be 71 or 72.

With that in mind, the audience must also be taken into account. Top of mind is that there is a range of roles involved and building consensus is at the heart of the process. A large scale does not support that goal as well as a smaller scale, with less of a range to pick from. The 100-point scale can be removed as an option, it is simply too wide, and the minute level of detail does not serve the desired purpose. The more technically-minded people would enjoy getting into the minor details and the executives would consider it a waste of time and create unnecessary friction. Added to that, the time needed to discuss at that level of detail would make it unwieldy and painful to work with.

On the other extreme is a 2-point rating system, basically a good versus bad or thumbs up versus thumbs down. The challenge here is that the excessive simplicity can mask opportunities to educate and communicate some of the issues being experienced. It almost negates the purpose of even having a scale at all. For that reason, there are three primary scales left to consider:

- 3-point scale
- 5-point scale
- 10-point scale

At this point, arguments can be made for each based on the scenario and people involved.

3-point scale

When time is of the essence and a very quick alignment is required or there are a large number of BVQs to score, the 3-point scale is preferable. It comes at the cost of specificity and an added risk of misalignment later in the process on account of a potential lack of conversation where some nuance may be needed.

5-point scale

Something of a happy medium, the 5-point scale provides a balance between speed and agility, with the ability to have more discussion where needed. It does take a little longer to reach consensus, but that overhead can also reduce risks later.

10-point scale

With the wider range comes greater depth of discussion but also the potential for wasting time on the minutia. Understanding the audience is important for this scale, more so than the others, because the time investment needed could frustrate some. For others, it may be just the amount of scale needed to be able to talk at the required technical depth.

Scoring the dimensions

When starting out, it is recommended to use the 3-point scale. When introducing a new concept or process, leaning on the side of efficiency, at the cost of accuracy, is an acceptable trade-off. People need to see it is fast and effective. Regardless, it is vastly more valuable to use the 3-point scale than not do the exercise at all, so there is already apparent benefit.

Once a degree of comfort is established, the scales could be used interchangeably on a per-BVQ basis. Leverage a 10-point scale where nuance and discussion is needed, and utilize the 3-point scale where speed is of the essence, and the question is already well understood and appreciated.

With the list of BVQs complete, the scoring can be applied to each one across the four dimensions of value, effort, cost, and data. Not all dimensions need to be scored all the time. One might elect to only focus on the data dimension initially during a first iteration. However, where time allows, there is a benefit to scoring across all four dimensions as discussion is enriched and hidden issues or challenges may be surfaced by so doing. Ultimately it comes down to what is achievable in the available time and balancing that with the impact on adoption. The balance is to determine what can acceptably be dropped on the current iteration and potentially picked up on a subsequent iteration.

Scoring the value dimension

For the non-technical participant, scoring BVQs by value will make immediate and relatable sense and is the ideal place to start when prioritizing. It also serves to highlight to more technical colleagues how important focusing on value is when working with data. While it is assumed that value is implicit in a BVQ, not all BVQs are made equal, and they have differing relative values when compared to each other.

Assuming the 3-point scale, a BVQ with 1 point in the value dimension would mean it has low relative value. A score of 3 would make it a high value consideration. A score of 2 suggests that it is reasonably valuable or that perhaps there is a mixed opinion as to the value. Value is in the eye of the beholder so a certain weighting must be given to the actual intended end user. A BI developer's view on what constitutes value may be correct but risk is introduced if the end user is not directly involved in determining what is value from their perspective. Not only that, but the stakeholder must also weigh in on this dimension.

Scoring the cost effectiveness dimension

The dimension of cost serves to highlight that extracting answers from data is not a magical formula, there are financial implications to every data and reporting request. If not already part of the equation, discussing cost can further educate stakeholders that there are financial considerations and emphasizes the importance of limiting requests to those with high value and high impact on the business.

As might be expected by now, a score of 1 for a given BVQ across the cost effectiveness dimension would imply the cost is not favorable. On the other end of the scale, at 3, the cost is either very favorable or negligible. A score of 2 is somewhere in between.

The challenge, of course, is that it may not be readily apparent how to calculate cost. While far from comprehensive, a quick way to achieve this is to estimate how much it costs to do the work. Consider the formula:

$$\text{People} \times \text{hours} \times \text{hourly rate}$$

Imagine for a certain BVQ it will take one data engineer approximately 40 hours to do the work. With an hourly rate of, for example, $95 then the equation would look like this:

$$1 \times 40 \times \$95 = \$3,800$$

We do not often think in terms of hard dollar costs, but it can be very sobering. Is the question so compelling that the cost can be justified? It does, at least, surface the topic for discussion and exploration. In addition, it may inform which BVQs are prioritized above others.

Scoring the ease of effort dimension

Effort can seem like a subset of cost. It can be, but it should also be considered separately. Breaking down the components of effort would include exploring the time it takes to perform the work, the effort needed to communicate it, any permission or security activities, as well as workflows or processes that need to be initiated.

The more that the level of effort can be exposed, the more awareness can be generated for how hard it often is when working with data. So, as with the other dimensions, there is an educational outcome to the scoring. Exposing the level of effort can be a little cumbersome at first as there will be the need to explain some of the details, but this will also serve to make it more relatable to people in subsequent iterations as well as gradually increase aspects of data literacy.

Effort is a little more ambiguous than the other dimensions. There will be potentially some "thumb in the air" estimating happening here. Even if there could be specificity, it is generally not desirable as it can make the process take longer. Consider where there is a set of 50 BVQs and you attempted to go into detailed estimating for each one in terms of effort. It would take a long time. Specificity will come later, and will be needed, but not prior to prioritization.

Like the cost effectiveness dimension, the scale is designed to where the low end means bad, and the high end is good. The rationale for this will become apparent during prioritization. A score of 1 across the ease of effort dimension, for a given BVQ, means it requires considerable effort, i.e., the ease of effort is low. Whereas a score of 3 is optimal, indicating not much effort is needed. Again, the score of 2 would suggest some effort if needed but it may be an acceptable amount.

Scoring the data dimension

As seen in the strategy template, there are many ways to measure the quality of underlying data sources, and those include, but are not limited to:

- missing
- incomplete
- does not exist
- unclean
- availability
- other

All of those are important but they are too technical for most businesspeople, and if building consensus is the goal that detail must be abstracted to a level of simplicity. To do this, just one score will be used for data. Assuming a 3-point scale, a score of 1 on the data dimension for a given BVQ would mean the data either does not exist or is in very bad shape in order to answer that BVQ. With a score of 3, the BVQ can be readily answered with the available data. A score of 2 would suggest that the data is in varying degrees of disarray and cannot be easily addressed. If in doubt, it is safer to round down. For example, if debating if a particular BVQ should have a data score of a 1 or 2, just go with the 1. The intent is to not spend too much time on scoring so that it becomes too burdensome to do at all. At this stage it is acceptable to trade accuracy for speed, but not too much accuracy that it becomes useless.

The bigger picture of scoring

Ideally, each BVQ will have four separate scores, one for each of the dimensions of value, cost, effort, and data. This gives an early indication of the viability of a BVQ and whether there is consensus across those four dimensions. A natural outcome of this effort is to question the purpose of including any BVQ that has a value score of 1. Indeed, there are certain patterns that may automatically exclude some BVQs, even before getting to prioritization. As an example, take a BVQ with the following scores:

Value: 1, Cost effectiveness: 1, Ease of effort: 1, Data: 1

The way to read this result is that it has little value, will be costly, and will take considerable effort as the data is either non-existent or of very poor quality. In short, why bother? On the other hand, a BVQ with the following score would be treated differently:

Value: 3, Cost effectiveness: 2, Ease of effort: 2, Data: 2

This score relates to high value with some moderate investment needed, it could take some time and effort, and the data is there but needs work, for example. Ultimately, each BVQ would have corresponding scores. The primary weighting is given to the value dimension as a means of simply weeding out low-value activities and saving needless effort on areas that do not impact the business.

When stated plainly, it sounds like common sense to not focus on low value. However, there is often not the opportunity to take a value-based perspective on how the data is being valued by the various roles involved.

Value is also relative to cost and effort. A question may be low value, but it might also be very easy to get to, i.e., low effort and no cost. In such a scenario it may still be desirable to include it.

These scores should foster discussion and an exchange of ideas. They form the foundation for a new way of building consensus and partnering. The framework is not complex and should be simple. The value is in the doing of it. Without question, there are more comprehensive ways of achieving the same results but if the approach is too cumbersome then it is less likely to be applied and consistently adopted. It is for this reason that not all dimensions need to be measured all the time. A rapid, though less comprehensive, approach that is actually applied is obviously preferable to a comprehensive approach that no one has the time or willingness to implement.

Zooming out to the bigger picture shows that the common points of misalignment and disagreement can start to be addressed at this early stage. These issues tend to only be surfaced much later in the data lifecycle, such as in user acceptance testing or, worse yet, after the launch. When surfaced in such a way, the friction is greater and the cost implications higher. On top of that, trust can be eroded, and adoption is the ultimate victim when failing to bring people on the journey.

If the project is to fail, it is preferable that it fails early, prior to any development proceeding. The activity of scoring can surface issues and points of friction that would normally only see the light of day during or after development. The hope is that, in a more controlled and structured setting, issues can be surfaced and systematically and proactively be addressed. It is partly why there are four dimensions, to maximize the opportunity to uncover as much as possible while still being agile.

STORY

Every project is different, the circumstances vary, and a degree of flexibility is often needed. In one such case, I was consulting for an energy company by teaching the BI team how to gather requirements. We were doing a real-world application by conducting the process of creating an executive end user persona and formulating the BVQs without having any time to talk to the target persona.

This was typical for the team, as getting a few hours with an executive was a challenge.

What we decided to do was to put our best foot forward and make some educated guesses of the persona, and we used that to inform the BVQs. The team were able to produce about 20 BVQs. Several on the team felt strongly about getting some face time with the executive in question. It looked like we could get 15 minutes with him and we wanted to make the very most of that time, so we came up with a plan.

On a whiteboard, we wrote the BVQs on sticky notes, one BVQ per sticky note. While we didn't know the value dimension for them, we could make a pretty good attempt at scoring the other dimensions. We used scoring dots, basically small circular stickers of various colors, to indicate the scores for each dimension.

The idea was to have all of these assembled on the whiteboard and the executive would come in and score the value dimension for each BVQ as well as identify any gaps. The executive came into the room and I gave him a 60-second overview of what we needed. He gave a quick overview of his top three goals and then we dove into the scoring activity. I gave an example of scoring one of them and he basically took over from there once he had grasped the purpose of the activity.

On the dot, after 15 minutes, he had to leave and said he really enjoyed the session and, if this was what the new BI process was going to look like, he would be happy to make 15 minutes available in the future when it was going to produce such high productivity. He joked about wishing all his meetings were like this.

The team were delighted, and the approach just clicked for most of them. While one of the goals was a little different from what the team had expected, it afforded the opportunity to identify two new BVQs that would support that goal.

The activity served to highlight that, with the right preparation, even a modicum of input from an end user can have a large impact on the project. Even with just those 15 minutes, the executive would later comment that he felt part of the design process and it gave him confidence in the team's ability to produce something he would use.

Prioritization of BVQs

Having gone through the steps to score each of the BVQs across the dimensions of value, cost effectiveness, ease of effort, and data, an initial pass at a prioritization can happen. The purpose of the activity is to find a balance between value and feasibility in an appropriate time frame. If it is the first iteration, emphasis might be placed differently to subsequent iterations. Perhaps establishing some quick wins is most important, so speed might be the guiding hand. In such a situation, BVQs with high ease of effort might be targeted and less focus placed on value.

There needs to be a guiding hand for any prioritization and that could change over time. Naturally, the value dimension is a preference, but it may be blocked by data quality or cost. Adding constraints can help narrow which dimensions to focus on. Some constraints to consider are time and number of BVQs. There might already be a deadline in place for releasing the dashboard, in which case only those BVQs that can be addressed in that timeline should be considered. However, the number of BVQs must be weighed also. There should not be too few where there is just one simple question being answered on the dashboard and the end user was expecting 50.

With the constraints of time, a target number of minimum BVQs, alongside the scoring, a reasonable attempt can be made to prioritize what should make it into the current iteration. There are several ways to go about this. A favorite is to use sticky notes and map them out on a whiteboard, either real or virtual. Each sticky note would have a single BVQ written on it. Of course, sticky notes are easily moved about, whatever framework is being leveraged.

One of the simplest frameworks is to map the BVQs on a basic matrix with the desired axes to highlight the dimensions that are most important. For example, the x-axis could be effort and the y-axis could be value. A BVQ in the top right quadrant would imply it is high value but also high effort. One in the top left would be high value but low effort, and these would likely be the ones to target first.

This gives a convenient visual way to assess the BVQ landscape, though it may be lacking in giving the whole picture as it only covers two dimensions. Another approach is to have multiple matrices that would cover all four of the dimensions. This would have duplication as each BVQ would be represented across two matrices, but has the added value of being able to see how a BVQ shapes out across multiple dimensions. For example, in addition to the previous grid, the second matrix might plot data quality on the x-axis and cost on the y-axis.

Another approach is to consolidate several dimensions into one. The dimensions of cost effectiveness, ease of effort, and data could be rolled into a single "feasibility" score. This new score could then be plotted against the value axis. In this case, a BVQ on the top right could suggest it is very feasible and has high value.

How the prioritization is visually represented depends on the criteria. If there is a tight timeline, then plotting value again ease of effort is preferable. If data quality and data cleanliness is a priority, then plotting value against the data dimension is the path forward. Perhaps value is not as important as building trust and keeping to a budget, in which case plotting the dimensions of data against cost effectiveness gives the desired context.

Whichever arrangement is used, a selection of a set of BVQs must be identified for the current iteration. Because of the scoring system and the selected matrix, those BVQs in the top right of the matrix are what should be considered first. For example, where the dimensions of value versus ease of effort were plotted, those sticky notes in the top right represent the highest value and with the least amount of effort to produce. Those are the most desirable items to prioritize as value and ease of effort were the identified criteria. The aim is to select the appropriate number of sticky notes, what can be completed in the prescribed amount of time for the current iteration.

Again, with a simplicity in mind, a circle can be drawn around the BVQs that are being considered. It serves as an easy means of facilitating discussion as to what questions are going to be answered and an early insight into what that might look like.

The journey so far

In order to have arrived at this point, with a prioritized list of business value questions, the path has had several interactions with various people and roles. Each interaction brought with it opportunities to increase adoption, from understanding the strategy and vision, to persona interviews, to determining the BVQs and prioritizing them. Communication has been at the heart of the process to date, and early attempts have been made to align the parties involved so far, as well as to paint a picture for those that will become involved later in the journey.

Believe it or not, this was the hard part. By taking all the steps to date, there will be significant reduction of risk, as many of the issues that impact adoption have already been reduced or managed, as much as possible. That is not to say that things will now progress smoothly, but a very solid foundation has been put in place by now. Everything that follows will be building on this foundation, so it is critical that it is well-formed by discussion and debate. If done properly, no one will be surprised, at least on a conceptual level, by the outputs once the dashboard is delivered.

If all someone had was this prioritized list of BVQs and the end-product dashboard, they could see a direct relationship between the BVQs and the visualizations. They would even likely see the exact questions detailed in the chart titles themselves. This is important because it is the glue that connects the technical and non-technical people across the common vision for what impact this data should have on the organization. It is this fabric that forms the shared understanding and collective expectations for what is to come.

06

The agile process

You may recall the story I related in Chapter 1, a client call in which we talked about how long an iteration of a dashboard would take. While I was being somewhat intentionally provocative about it, I did not really expect to win the work. Indeed, it was not enough for the client to go off either. There were plenty of other firms to choose from that were more aligned with their way of doing things. But they felt there was something there and they devised a cunning plan.

They were going to have a real-world mini challenge of one iteration of a dashboard and have their favorite firms compete over the period of a week. Whichever team produced the most valuable dashboard would win a large book of business. They understood the value of adoption, and that it takes time, but this exercise was to observe the speed of development.

The setup was to deliver the requirements at the start of the week, Monday, in a two-hour meeting where all the firms would attend. One hour would be given for stating the requirements and the second hour was to be a questions and answers session. Following that meeting, the teams would be given an extract of data in the form of a spreadsheet. The teams would have until the end of the week, Friday, to build out the dashboard and present it back.

It was all fast paced, with little notice, and I had a prior engagement that kept me out on Monday and Tuesday. Unable to attend the requirements session, I requested that we do a mini requirements workshop for an hour on Wednesday afternoon. Fortunately, the client agreed, and we started to prep. However, that only gave a couple of days to work on it. To be continued....

The historic approach

In times past, the reporting lifecycle would follow the waterfall project management methodology. The approach takes a project and breaks it up into discrete and sequential stages. A stage can only start once the prior stage has completed, and each stage is generally not revisited once it is complete. The approach is known for not being flexible to change and longer project durations. However, the roles are clearly understood, and the lack of change makes it easier to navigate.

Given the impact that data can have on people and an organization, the lack of feedback and inflexibility to change makes the waterfall methodology less than ideal for data projects that involve an end user interface. It can still be appropriate for data work on the backend, such as a data migration to the cloud or large technology transformations where there is a linear and sequential process that, once it is done is done, i.e., no steps need to be revisited once complete.

Though there is some variation, the waterfall approach is typically broken down into several steps:

1 Requirements: gathering of requirements for the project.

2 Design: design of the system based on the requirements.

3 Implementation: development of the system based on the design.

4 Testing: testing to find and address any bugs and issues.

5 Deployment: delivery of the completed project.

6 Maintenance: address on-going issues and bugs.

The stages of the waterfall approach sound very reasonable and logical. The challenge, however, is that it might not be able to move at the pace the business needs. From one moment to the next, some data might provide insight that would require a change in business strategy. That change should quickly feed back into the business and into the dashboards and reports that are being used so that they can realign with the new strategy, where appropriate. By and large, it is more difficult to have this level of flexibility with waterfall alone.

With the long periods of time from stage to stage, the waterfall methodology requires extensive documentation, otherwise known as "the spec." Not a lot of people like reading a 150-page specification document, and even fewer enjoy writing it! But it is necessary in order for the approach to work. If there are changes to requirements then they must be extensively documented because the cost of change is significant due to the development often being underway already, due to the lack of flexibility to gather feedback and be agile.

The waterfall framework was originally created for the production line, namely by Henry Ford when he optimized the assembly line that broke the production process into a series of clear steps so that the end-result vehicle would closely match the design specification. It made a lot of sense to leverage that for projects that did not change much, i.e., the spec for a Ford vehicle was fixed for a set amount of time, and did not rapidly change. In the 1970s, the approach was formalized for software development and it was a success as it provided a clear specification to follow. Back then, software requirements would also change slowly due to the technical complexity of the systems and the relative slow speed of the underlying systems.

With the advent of the internet, mixed with capitalism, there was pressure to create applications that could get to market faster. Getting to market faster, even by a few weeks, could make or break a startup. Added to the mix were smaller teams than usual as well as team members that did not have a traditional computer science background, so more flexibility was needed away from the more monolithic practices.

The agile approach

BI and analytics are in a unique position in that their function is to accurately reflect the real world. For this, a specific, off-the-shelf process will not have the required mix of agility while also managing change and bringing people along for the journey. A blend of short-term flexibility must also be partnered with the longer-term needs of change management.

However, there already is a great starting point with the agile project management approach that leverages an iterative process. Many organizations are already using the methodology and even have their own dedicated teams for managing projects in this way. The agile approach was originally conceived for better management of software development projects. Indeed, it was a team of 17 technologists and software developers that put their heads together and came up with the "Manifesto for agile software development". Almost revolutionary at the time, but taken as common sense now, the manifesto places value on these four principles:

1 Individuals and interactions over processes and tools

2 Working software over comprehensive documentation

3 Customer collaboration over contract negotiation

4 Responding to change over following a plan

Each principle expresses a preference. For example, with the second principle, it is not that there should be no documentation, but having a functional dashboard is more important and should take priority over creating a 300-page document. While intended for software development, there is considerable overlap and value in adapting these principles to the realm of data. Indeed, there is a large degree of similarity when software and dashboards are viewed as products.

There are several interesting concepts shared in these concise principles and they speak to volumes of experience in failed waterfall projects. Rather than start from scratch, the agile approach provides a very rich and fertile soil in which to grow out a methodology more suited to delivering insight. By way of adapting an existing best practice, an exploration of how each principle can be adapted to BI is necessary.

Individuals and interactions over processes and tools

While process is important, its value should lie in how it brings people along the journey. A process should allow for interactions and support adaptation when feedback suggests it. Process is also important in how it can give step-by-step directions in when and how to have those people interactions. It views process as a people enabler and not process just as a means to build a dashboard. When process is viewed in such a way it places the emphasis where it should be.

The same is true for tools. In the BI world, far too much emphasis has been given to tools as a means to address problems that have their roots in misaligned people. Misdiagnosing a people problem as a tool problem is commonplace in the field. For example, self-service tools are offered to increase adoption or provide great access to insight for end users. However, the problem could be solved by having greater, or more pointed, interaction with the end users to deliver something of value to them. Certainly, the right tool is important but, without people on board, it is largely a waste of money.

The moral of the story with this principle is that people are at the heart of the story and they need to be interacted with as humans and not as part of some transactional process.

Working software over comprehensive documentation

More of a problem for larger software development projects, there can be a significant documentation burden, such as a system requirements specification. The notion here is that, while documentation is important, it is better to have an intuitive and functional interface that provides value in a shorter amount of time versus taking longer to build the interface and having extensive documentation. With documentation, the "time to market" is longer and can take away from the value of just getting something in front of people to react to.

It is similar to the concept of "failing fast"—if the users don't respond well then not a lot of time was wasted in producing needless documentation, since it would have to change anyway. The idea is to build quickly, get something in front of the users, and see what they think. With the right approach, this can end up being much faster to get to market by dealing with bite-size chunks over short periods of time and validating each chunk. In addition, it is considerably lower risk than waiting until everything is complete before getting user feedback.

Customer collaboration over contract negotiation

This principle places emphasis on close collaboration and partnership between the parties as a means to maintain tight alignment on expectations and outcomes. Obviously, with limited collaboration, nailing the details of the scope and requirements up front becomes important because they are used as the north star for the entirety of the engagement. Changes to that north star then require change requests to update or amend the original documentation. There are pros and cons to this, but for the purposes of BI and analytics it is preferable to follow the agile approach and favor close collaboration.

As with the other principles, it is not one or the other, but a weighting is given to collaboration while there can still be an appropriate level of contract negotiation if the project calls for it.

Responding to change over following a plan

For analytics and BI purposes, the last principle sings especially true: responding to change over following a plan. Having a 12-month or 24-month plan, without flexibility, can absolutely decimate an organization's data culture. However, a plan, at the right level, can be a good thing. So long as that plan can be malleable to changes in the project lifecycle. It also depends on how strategic the plan is. If it is more outcomes-based and deals less with the tactical application, then it can be easier to maintain that plan. Conversely, if it is very detailed and gets into the weeds, the more likely it is that it will need to be changed and adjusted.

Being inflexible causes its own issues that can exceed the benefit of having a fixed plan. The reality is that change will happen. The longer the plan, the more that change will occur. By accepting this, and adopting the right methodology, the journey can be lower in friction and more productive for all involved.

Rolling the agile principles together

In summary, the agile framework provides a solid foundation for how to run and manage analytics projects. It is a modern approach to how to adjust to the speed of both the business and the market. It was originally formed for software development and, while there is considerable overlap, the framework needs work if it is to be applied to the realm of BI and analytics. To move in that direction, it can be beneficial to look at the outputs of such a project in terms of a living and breathing entity.

The living dashboard

A dashboard needs to be a living thing. It is a living thing because it is associated with a persona and that persona has changing needs as the business changes. In the world around us, living things can only survive with a feedback loop. It must be the same for a dashboard. It lives and breathes the business, the environment the business is in, and adjusts accordingly. The external stimuli allow it to grow and adjust and it provides a window into that world for the end user. Without that change, the end user will be looking at an incorrect representation of the world and their decisions will be similarly misguided.

There is a species of warrior ant that, like many other ants, uses a chemical signal to track members of their own colony. Some of those ants have figured out how to mimic the signal given off from another colony. This allows them to attack the colony and more easily take control. Even more remarkable, the worker ants of the colony being attacked will not even realize that they are under attack and will continue working! They do not have an appropriate feedback loop in place that can update their model of reality.

While unaware of it, many businesses and departments are experiencing this situation. They lack the feedback loop and are unable to have a response. Some extreme examples of that are Blockbuster and Sears. It was no guarantee that having the feedback loop would have saved many of those closures, but there may have been greater opportunity to shift the business model in response to the changed environment.

A dashboard needs two feedback loops. The first is the feedback from the world. Is it accurately reflecting what is going on out in the environment? The second is the feedback loop with the end users. Is it adapting to the changing needs they have? More simply put, a dashboard is a feedback loop to the business while also allowing it to reflect an accurate view of the world. Therefore, any process that is to be leveraged for creating dashboards must have these feedback loops at their core.

Achieving this mighty feat requires a step-by-step, easily understood, and simple to apply process. It needs to be quick to react to change yet still have consistency in how it is delivered. As Bruce Lee is famous for saying "Be water, my friend." Adapt to the situation. The vision is for a framework that can act like water and become the shape of whatever vessel it is poured into with agility and value yet still maintain a forward movement following a path or plan.

The stages of a successful process

With the working principles for a framework for analytics and BI adoption already established, it is time to focus on how those principles can be enacted through a step-by-step process. The process should be able to scale for when a very light application is needed or expand to be very deep when considerable detail is necessary. For that reason, the process can be viewed initially from the following high-level stages:

1 Requirements
2 Design
3 Build
4 Adoption

Each stage has its own sub stages or steps within them. Each stage can, and oftentimes should, iterate upon itself several times before moving on to the next stage. Each stage builds on the previous one and is generally going to be constrained by the outputs from that prior stage. However, each stage can be revisited or iterated upon before moving to the next stage. Visit the book website to download a printable version of the process.

The entire process repeats over the iterations of the dashboard as more data becomes available and more advanced analytics are applied to the model. The process allows for this flexible expansion and evolution. In every stage there is opportunity for end user and stakeholder engagement so that the story of the data can be continuously shared, and feedback gathered. Before exploring the individual steps in each stage, it is valuable to explore the purpose of each stage first.

Requirements

This stage places an emphasis on people and understanding the needs of the business. It is covered in detail in Chapters 4 and 5. This is a poorly understood and underutilized set of steps that go a long way to increasing adoption. This stage enables the first interactions with the various parties involved, with the opportunity to indicate that it will not be business as usual. The steps in this stage include:

1 Strategy: completing the strategy template

2 Interviews: structured interviews with the end users

3 Personas: distilling the interviews into personas

4 Questions: identifying the BVQs

5 Assessment: conducting the data assessment against the BVQs

6 Prioritization: determining the BVQs to be addressed

7 Iteration roadmap: assigning BVQs to each iteration

Depending on scale and speed, anywhere from one of the steps to all of them might be completed in this stage. As to which ones are most important, experience suggests that step 1, strategy, is the most critical. The reason for this is that it provides the context and value for the dashboard. Without it, everything else becomes somewhat transactional. It is challenging to determine what other steps should be taken if time is limited. They are simply all incredibly important to the success of a BI project, especially at this early stage. However, if it is a second or subsequent iteration of the same project, then it is certainly easier to reduce which steps are needed, on a case-by-case basis.

Saying all that, there is an efficient way of bringing all these steps together in a facilitated workshop. It does take a degree of planning and preparation but can be a highly effective way of bringing people along for the journey in the quickest possible way while still ensuring value. However, facilitating such a workshop is not for the faint of heart or for someone inexperienced in facilitation. For the first few times of leveraging these steps it is better to take them one at a time and develop a degree of comfort with them prior to bringing them all together in a workshop.

Indeed, running all these steps in a workshop is often preferable and more impactful. Depending on the scope, and number of people involved, a requirements workshop of this type can take anywhere from two hours to three days, the typical session being in the four-hour range on account of availability of the participants and scheduling issues.

The preference of the author is to have three primary steps; complete the strategy template with the stakeholder(s), conduct the interviews with the end users, and then facilitate a workshop for the remainder of the steps with the prep for the workshop including the outputs from the interviews and the creation of the personas. With some experience, this becomes a rapid process that can quickly align the participants, especially if they have been through it before and know what to expect.

Design

The second stage covers design and attempts to produce the first visuals for the end user to react to. There is still no development, or any code being written. The goal of this stage is to take the requirements, for the chosen iteration, and distill them from questions into a dashboard format. This includes breaking BVQs down into KPIs, selecting the right charts, and determining the associated actions. It is the visual translation of "So what?"

A common challenge for analytics is that an end user often only sees their first visuals for a dashboard once it has already been developed. That is far too late in the process. They may not react favorably to what they see, and rework may be necessary. That rework may be costly, depending on the level of effort required and the tools being used. The preference is to still give something the end user can react to, but make it lightweight and quick to make changes to. This is accomplished with a wireframe. Wireframes will be covered in depth later in the book, but, briefly, a wireframe is an efficient means of giving a visual representation of what the output will look like, without the need for development effort.

The result is that the end user will have something to react to and to give feedback on, prior to starting development. If needed, changes can be made to the design so that the end user is satisfied, and their expectations are set according to the outputs of the requirements stage. Breaking down the steps of the design stage includes:

8 Tab formation: grouping BVQs into dashboard tabs

9 KPI definition: identification of KPIs

10 Scenario mapping: assigning actions and visuals to BVQs

11 Wireframing: visualizing the desired end state

12 Feedback: gathering end user feedback

13 Documentation: light documentation for the project

Like the other stages, it is optional which steps to follow. Of course, the ideal is that all the steps would be taken but that may not be possible. While each of these steps will be covered in detail in subsequent chapters, the most impactful step to take is scenario mapping, as it can concisely take a BVQ and extract the KPIs and associated visual and map them to actions. However, wireframing is a close second place here so both are recommended when in a pinch.

This stage can have heavy interaction with the end user as a feedback loop to ensure the requirements have been correctly interpreted and the expectations are aligned. Between the requirements and design stages, the risk and friction can be more easily managed, with the necessary changes quickly iterated upon. To progress from this stage, it is recommended to have some acknowledgement, whether formal or informal, that there will not be significant changes once development starts. Otherwise, it somewhat defeats the purpose of producing the wireframes and gathering feedback.

Build

For many BI developers, the temptation is to start development right away, once a request for a new dashboard has come in, the requirements for which might have been vague and poorly thought out. The intent can be virtuous, such as checking whether the data is there to support the request or perhaps in an attempt to just get the job done as fast as possible. Without the requirements and design stages, the BI developer has very little to go off. The likely outcome is that the dashboard might solve an immediate need but there will probably be more ad hoc requests from the same requestor and there will be little more use for the previous dashboard.

It is difficult to break the cycle, but development should only be started once a baseline degree of requirements has been gathered and there is a wireframe to follow, that the requestor has seen and agreed with. A trade is being made to exchange ad hoc requests for more partnership for requirements in return for higher value, longer lived dashboards.

The stages of dashboard development are generally well understood and do not require revisiting in this book. What is important, however, is the handoff from the requirements and design stages and how they should be interpreted by the developer(s). The steps in this stage of the process include:

14 Interpretation: understanding the outputs from the previous stages

15 Data model: design and build of the model in support of the wireframes

16 Performance: tuning and tailoring of the speed of the user experience

17 Dashboard build: development of the dashboard

18 User acceptance testing: end user feedback and associated tweaks

This stage is also cyclical but the number of cycles should be based on the minor changes identified from UAT and not changes to requirements or design—that ship should have already sailed for this iteration. If the participants have been involved appropriately in the prior stages, their expectations should already be aligned on what is in scope and out of scope for the development stage.

Adoption

The final stage in the process is intentionally named adoption. The reasoning is to make no bones about what the intent of the dashboard should be: adoption. Quite often, the final stage is development and little thought is given to what follows. The term "build it and they will come" is unfortunately not going to work as well for analytics and BI as it did in the movie *Field of Dreams*. However, that is often the notion that developers have, even if they do not consciously think that. Their work is done and now people should use it. However, adoption requires effort and a plan.

The adoption stage assumes the job is not done and that development, by itself, is only going to be sufficient in a certain set of scenarios. For most situations, a degree of effort and energy will be needed to get the work across the finish line and to bring the participants along the journey until the desired number of end users are engaging with the outputs. Naturally, a degree of assessment and measurement is required to track whether the stated, desired outcomes from the start of the iteration are being achieved.

19 Training materials: sufficient training content to enable the end users

20 Pilot: if necessary, a small pilot launch to test adoption

21 Launch plan: execution of a launch sequence to drive adoption

22 Measurement: tracking against the stated goals and outcomes

23 Next iteration: planning and adjustments for the next iteration

Upon completion of this stage, it may be necessary to adjust the goals and outcomes for the next iteration based on the feedback from the current iteration. Perhaps there were issues that surfaced that require reprioritization on the next iteration. Perhaps business priorities changed during the course of the process. Whatever the case, change is normal, and the process must be able to flex and adjust accordingly.

Bringing it all together

With each stage being iterative, it makes sense that the whole process itself is also iterative. Each iteration building on the last. What this entails is a regular cadence and scheduling of each iteration, to help with planning as well as sating expectations for the end users and stakeholders. The time between iterations allows for work to be done on improving data quality, acquiring new data sources, cleansing, etc. That time between the release of iterations must be long enough to achieve a number of outcomes:

- Support the next priority BVQs with making the necessary data available.
- Allow for end users to adjust to the previous iteration.
- Measurement and assessment of goals in the previous iteration.

However, it does not mean that the process just stops at the end of the last iteration and goes on pause for a set amount of time. The next iteration can start immediately. What is not desirable is that the next iteration is released to production immediately, without having time for the end users to experience the previous iteration. All that being said, there is a balance to be maintained. This balance depends on the organization and situation. It is the balance of taking long enough between releases to have meaningful change but short enough so end users and stakeholders can see that progress is being made. An aspect of why the process works is the realistic setting of expectations. The reality is that all the questions an end user has can probably not be immediately answered based on available data. The process allows that request to be broken up into iterations. To say "Yes" to the request but to also say it is a journey. If the gap between iterations is too long, it may no longer be perceived as a journey. Again, depending on the situation, starting the next iteration quickly will show the participants that progress is being made and there is a predictable cadence and the opportunity to give more input.

The next iteration is an experience for the end user. It does not mean starting development right away. It means starting with the first steps, the strategy. Does the strategy need to adjust after the learnings from the previous iteration? It likely does. Have the goals of the business shifted? Did the last iteration make a big enough impact that the needle has moved for the business? One cannot assume business as usual. Indeed, if the promise of analytics is realized, then the strategy should change. It is an important differentiator from the typical waterfall approach.

Chances are that much of the strategy is good and just some changes are needed. These changes might inform the next stages of the process, such as the interviews, personas, and BVQs. There might be a reprioritization of the BVQs. At least there is an opportunity for changes to happen. Even if they do not happen at every iteration, there is an understood flexibility to adjust as needed.

There is a scene in the movie *The 13th Warrior*, set in the Viking era, where a boy arrives on a ship in front of a Viking encampment. The boy stands on the prow of the ship for several hours. The reason given is that, because it is an unexpected occurrence, he stands there to show that he is real, that he exists. Basically, he gives the encampment the courtesy of adjusting to the change and the new reality of a ship being present before their eyes. They are given the time to think about it. This process has a similar impact. With the iterative approach, and the predictive nature of the steps, invites can be sent to end users for interviews and feedback. Even if those invites are far into the future, it is setting the expectation that they will continue to be involved and their feedback valued. They can adjust. They can think about what is to come and how it can impact their own reality.

A degree of comfort is engendered, and iterations establish routine and a sense of calm, i.e., the end user doesn't have to think of absolutely everything they need in any given iteration or their chance is lost. The fear of missing out or needing to put things off until complete can be mitigated. They know there will be continuous opportunities to engage and have their voice heard. It is part of the reason why the iterations are plotted to a basic timeline in the strategy template, so this schedule can be shared with the end users at every opportunity.

Application

At first glance, the entire process appears to have a lot of steps! It can seem burdensome and overly comprehensive to follow every single step, every single time, for every iteration. The practical reality is that every step is not always needed and is dependent on the situation. Naturally, the first time through an iteration will take a little more time, particularly if people are new to the process. That applies to both lack of familiarity in applying the process but also people experiencing it for the first time. Due to that, time must be allotted for adjustment.

When introducing a new process, the preference may be to not apply all the steps right away and introduce additional steps through subsequent iterations. To become comfortable with the process, it can be prudent to limit the scope of the project and how many people will be involved. Potentially even starting with just one end user. Some tweaks may need to be made and perhaps not every step is applicable to the organization. This little test application will help build comfort with the process and make any necessary adjustments. Confidence in applying the process is key. You must appear to know what you are doing and to be able to back that up with experience, even if that experience is short, but there needs to be something behind it.

The ideal situation is to apply the process for the first time on a low-risk project. The number of end users would be limited, and the stakeholders would be advocates for change. Just like learning a new skill, focus can first be placed on the steps and how to do them. In such an environment, mistakes can be made, and lessons learned, before applying the approach to more strategic and impactful higher-risk projects.

As previously stated, many organizations produce dashboards at breakneck speed, and that may be appropriate. At some point, however, that speed may not allow the end user to think strategically. The flip side is that the development team will continue to be reactive, just responding to requests and unable to stick their heads out of the water and get the wider perspective. It raises the often-asked question, how long should an iteration take?

Iteration duration

It depends. There are several constraints that can impact the duration of an iteration, such as how this process can fit into an organization's current project management approach. If there are weekly sprints, then that must be considered. If there are constraints on resources or people availability, then these must be accounted for. All of those aside, there are some general rules of thumb that are worthy of consideration.

First, each stage can be considered a sprint. That would mean an iteration of a dashboard would take four weeks. It is a reasonable amount of time but is recommended for lower-risk dashboards where speed is required.

A second option is to iterate even faster and fit the entire process into a two-week sprint. What inevitably suffers is the adoption stage because it is challenging to compress that any more than it already is, but such is the reality of the enterprise!

Finally, where the risks are higher and time allows for it, taking three months per iteration affords the balance between being comprehensive and ensuring greater chances of adoption. Much longer than that and some of the downsides of the waterfall approach start to rear their heads.

Ultimately, it depends on what works for the organization, and what parts of the process are more important and what can be sacrificed. It is not an all-or-nothing situation. Doing part of the process is already an improvement over not doing any of it. Indeed, doing all of it may be inappropriate for the organization and speed of business. Regardless, many organizations have struggled with the issue of what to do when priorities change during a process. Especially if the process is a long one.

STORY

There was a specific project that had an unusual winning criterion for some work I won. It is typical in the consulting world for several vendors to be considered when an organization wants support with a project. In this instance, the main criterion for selection was, how does the team respond to client change requests? Not being a fan of excessive documentation, my response is that change requests are not needed because change is built into the process. There is no need to have a formal change request process because it slows things down and no one likes documentation.

Honestly, I thought they would consider that a little bit too loose for them and having a paper trail was necessary. However, it turned out that they had been dealing with another consulting firm that was doing exactly that, i.e., having the client fill out a change request form every time they wanted to make even minor tweaks. The client was sick of it and wanted a lighter way to give feedback and change course during a project. Thankfully, they decided to go with the lighter approach.

Change requests

Change requests primarily happen for one of two reasons; things changed during development or the end user's expectations were not properly aligned during the project inception and requirements stage. There are other factors, but these are the main scenarios that are encountered. The former is exacerbated by long development cycles. The latter is due to little or no formal requirements process.

With development cycles being shorter in this process, the potential for change requests is already reduced. In addition, through shorter iteration cycles, change requests can be considered feedback for the next iteration and should be treated as such unless there is some compelling rationale to the contrary.

With an abundance of opportunity for end user and stakeholder input and engagement throughout the process, the need for changes is greatly reduced. Indeed, a more compelling argument can be made to push back against change requests, as they are likely due to the requestor not participating in the process to start with. By design, the process should alleviate the need for a majority of typical change requests.

Start now

The process is a nice theoretical concept until it is actually put into practice. Even if the situation is not ideal, and all the chess pieces are not exactly in place as hoped for, it is better to start with some parts of the process. One of the lowest-friction options is to just add wire-framing to the current approach and, bit by bit, add more and more of the steps from the process.

The following chapters of the book will focus on the remaining stages of the process that have been outlined in this chapter. In the next chapter, the exciting world of dashboard design and storytelling is going to be explored in depth.

Reference

Beck, K., Beedle, M., van Bennekum, A., Cockburn, A., Cunningham, W., Fowler, M., Grenning, J., Highsmith, J., Hunt, A., Jefferies, R., Kern, J., Marick, B., Martin, R. C., Mellor, S., Schwaber, K., Sutherland, J., Thomas, D. 2001. Manifesto for agile software development. https://agilemanifesto.org/ (archived at https://perma.cc/LG9B-QQDA)

07

Storytelling

STORY

When I started working in data visualization I would keep hearing the term "storytelling" and how important it is. I had my own notion of what storytelling meant. Having grown up in Ireland, storytelling brought back memories of people in pubs re-telling great stories from myths and legends. There was an art to it. Much depended on the charisma of the storyteller and their ability to engage the audience with the tone and pace of their voice. It was thrilling to watch and listen to!

I thought that storytelling was something I could never do, especially with my notion of what it meant. I was to learn that not everyone shared that view of what was entailed in storytelling, and that there was not really a common and shared appreciation for what telling stories with data meant. To this day, I think there is still a misconception about what it means.

I'm not saying it is a right or agreed upon version of what storytelling is or should be, but the approach I have found to work is most effective when embedded into a process and to have a formulaic approach to it. By placing an emphasis on structure over art, and process over creativity, it is much more accessible and practical for enterprise application and, ultimately, adoption.

This became most evident to me when I had the opportunity to work on a data journalism project. In such a situation, one has several benefits. The data is fixed in time, it is historical. We know the message we are trying to share. Data quality issues are already managed. Basically, it is a very safe and easy way to make a story. Imagine telling the story of the spread of malaria through a large region. The story can be very compelling and follow a narrative. But, what happens when you want to do the same in the enterprise? Data is changing regularly, the business is changing, there are data issues and there could be any number of competing issues that need attention. It took me a long time, but I eventually gave up on trying to apply the same standards for storytelling that could be used in the data journalism example.

I felt like I was pretty mediocre at storytelling and was a good average representation for how people thought about the topic. If I was struggling with it, then I was sure others were too, so I decided to do something about it. With the process already being successful for adoption, I started to experiment with how to add the "storytelling" element into it.

Why do we need to be able to tell stories with data? Why is storytelling such a common term in the field of data? It is a means to convey meaning and context to a set of data. More specifically, through supporting visualizations, a narrative can be built that helps the user to take some sort of action.

Compelling storytelling with data in the enterprise can be difficult. It truly depends on the definition used for storytelling and the expectations for what that means. We are all used to the typical story and narrative structure used in the movie industry. It goes something like this:

1 Meet the characters

2 Something dramatic happens to the characters

3 There is a struggle

4 Things get resolved

Most movies fit into some variation of that storyline and it generally works pretty well, albeit somewhat predictably. There are many versions of the story arc, but a popular one is the formula created by Kenn Adams. It is called the Story Spine and it looks like this:

1 Once upon a time there was _____

2 Every day, _____

3 One day _____

4 Because of that, _____

5 Because of that, _____

6 Until finally _____

Obviously, the blanks are to be filled in, but a very wide range of stories can be crafted with this structure. A former storyboard artist at Pixar, a company known for telling great stories, Adams breaks it down with these following questions. Why must you tell this story? What is the belief burning within you that your story feeds off of? What greater purpose does this serve? What does it teach?

It is probably becoming evident that this concept of storytelling might be great for movies and books, but it does not naturally map over to the world of data and telling stories through that medium in a similar way. This is where there can be a disconnect between what traditional storytelling does and what storytelling using data should be.

Perhaps a more traditional view is the story arc. It comprises of the exposition, rising action, climax, falling action, and ends with resolution. The exposition is the introduction and exposes the audience to the key themes and the characters. Who are the characters and how can they be differentiated? The mood is also set in the exposition.

The rising action is when something happens that breaks from the normal. It is the start of conflict. In the movie *Jaws*, the rising action begins when the first attack happens at the beach. We start to learn more about the characters and what the impacts are.

The climax builds the tension to the point where something happens at the peak. It is the veritable moment of truth. In *Jaws*, it is the moment that the shark is killed. (On a side note, the author's father once lived near Robert Shaw, who played Quint in *Jaws*!) The falling action is where any remaining actions need to be taken and untied ends can be closed off. It is the bridge from the climax to the resolution stage. Not quite the end yet, but things are starting to wrap up.

Finally, there is the resolution. It is the end of the story and a good place to bring closure and share any lessons learned. One could see how this is a little more applicable to our needs. What is especially interesting is the term "resolution".

The story arc applied to insight

The phrase "actionable outcomes" gets thrown around a lot in analytics. What is that other than the desire to reach some sort of resolution, through taking action? The concept is to use data to bring matters to a resolution. For example, a dashboard indicates that a certain product is low on inventory. The action is to order more inventory. The resolution is that there is now enough stock. It is the resolution that is being sought after. It boils down to: a problem is noticed, the problem is understood, action is taken, and the problem is resolved.

Attempting to fit that to the story arc structure, it might look a little like this:

- Exposition: product inventory levels are being checked.
- Rising action: inventory levels appear to be off a little.
- Climax: low inventory for a specific product is identified.
- Falling action: order of additional inventory.
- Resolution: inventory levels are now normal.

What is interesting here is that the story arc does not necessarily all occur within the dashboard interface. Specifically, the falling action stage would likely happen elsewhere. It may be a phone call to an operations team to place an order, it might be entering the order into an ordering system interface, etc. The point is, part of the story arc, for it to work, is likely not confined just to the dashboard. However, the challenge can be in tracking that action and how it brings the story to closure and resolution in the dashboard. That is, how does the end user know that the action taken has resulted in the desired resolution, if that action is taken outside of the current user experience?

The circle of the story must be closed. In the context of reporting and BI, the story arc concept has some merit. Of course, this only applies to operational and tactical type reporting and dashboarding.

It is not applicable to data exploration in the same way and the approach in this chapter will not work for such applications. There is a degree of structure needed in order for the basic framework of climax, action, and resolution to make any degree of repeatable sense. More on tracking of actions later.

Storytelling with acts

Another way to look at storytelling is using acts. William Shakespeare's plays always followed an act structure. He used the five-act narrative structure that was taken from the ancient Greeks and it maps closely to the story arc structure. For greater simplification, breaking it down into an even simpler structure, there are three acts for the story to play out, in a similar way to the story arc.

- Act 1 sets the scene, introduces the characters, and reveals the elements that could go wrong or where problems might be looming.
- Act 2 expands on the problems, and the characters change and adjust to the evolving situation. There is conflict and it comes to a climax in this act.
- Act 3 brings the resolution; the characters are happy and balance is restored.

STORY

Growing up in Ireland, any chance to get to watch an American TV show was a major highlight. One of those shows, though maybe not entirely suitable for kids, was *The Streets of San Francisco*, with the then rising star of Michael Douglas and the already celebrated Karl Malden. It had very memorable shots of the Bay area in the opening credits and the music would instantly transport me into the world of investigation that the show was about. In my mind, the defining feature of San Francisco was the hills and how the streets had great inclines to them, which made for very dramatic chase scenes.

Something else that stood out to me was how the producer, Quinn Martin, broke every episode up into a series of acts, starting with Act 1, and wrapped up the episode with an epilogue. While all the action had finished, the epilogue had the effect of nicely wrapping up the show and provided any moral lessons related to the action. The net effect was that I knew what to expect from each act, which gave me a sense of comfort and familiarity with the show that may not have been there otherwise.

The three-act structure lends itself well to a need for simplicity but also it is easier to apply than the other story structures out there, especially for people without a background in storytelling. This structure will be used as the basis for the structure of the dashboard where a narrative can play out.

The challenge of enterprise storytelling

Simply having a structure for a narrative does not mean a narrative will play out within a dashboard every time it is viewed. Since the focus is on operational and tactical type dashboards, the story is dependent on what is going on with the data on any given day.

This is the challenge with storytelling with data, the misconceptions with what it is, and how to do it. As has been previously stated, when several factors are controlled, such as a specific date range, a specific population or other dimension, and there is limited filtering, such as in data journalism, it is quite straightforward to create a story if there is a story to be told. However, as is often the case in the enterprise, there is a moving target. The more dimensions there are to filter, the harder it is to manage a clear narrative.

There can be a desire to put as many filters into a dashboard as there are dimensions in the data. While that can be useful at times, it can complicate a narrative structure. To address the challenge, the number of dimensions needs to be limited as well as gaining a degree of control over the visual elements of a dashboard. As many elements need to be controlled as possible in order for there to be sufficient narrative pathways. This is achieved through several means, all of which must work together:

- An appropriately scoped end user persona—the narrower the persona then the easier it is to build a narrative for what they care about.
- Clear and simple goals with well-defined and understood resultant actions.
- A dashboard layout that groups context-related BVQs together in one tab.
- The appropriate use of filters, charts, and KPIs.

Even with all the above, there is still no guarantee of a clear story coming through. The idea is to create pathways for narratives to happen. For example, taking the product inventory scenario, what if everything is fine; inventory levels are where they should be. There is no story there, other than that there is no story, i.e., life is good and there is no action to take. The design is scenario-based with the scenarios being tied to business outcomes and the desired goals. As such, the dashboard becomes a vehicle for taking actions, when there is misalignment, to progress towards a goal. Broadly speaking, the story is the journey that the end user takes to realize both their goals and the goals of the business. The end user undertakes a veritable odyssey on the path to achieving the strategic goals set out at the project inception, though hopefully it doesn't take the ten years it took Odysseus to return home!

Translating acts to dashboards

Now we have an appreciation for what storytelling is and its applicability to dashboards and data, how can it be manifested in a dashboard and what are the benefits of so doing? People tend to not have a lot of free time to go clicking all over a dashboard to find any nuggets that might be in there. A clear call to action needs to be front and center. What action can I take if I have a spare five minutes in my day? The dashboard presents that opportunity to support the end user in such a way and using the story narrative structure is conducive to doing that effectively. Executed well, a dashboard quickly gives the end user context, whether that be historical or otherwise (Act 1), in order to highlight any outliers or items that need attention (Act 2). Thus enabling the end user with the actions they need to take to bring resolution (Act 3).

Act 1 is the content of the dashboard. What are the names of the dashboard's tabs, what metrics, charts, and filters are grouped together? What are the chart titles? In combination, these features introduce the story, the background to what is going to unfold.

Act 2 is the highlight in the dashboard. Is something red or orange? Is there an outlier calling for attention? Where is it not business as usual? The reason for the highlight is easily understood and stands out from the rest of the content. Of course, there must be sufficient context for the highlight to make sense.

Act 3 requires that there must be a clear call to action in relation to the highlight. There needs to be a path or workflow that can address the highlight. Beyond that, a means of tracking the impact of that action is necessary to ensure it was the right action to take in order to achieve resolution.

There is a direct relationship between each act and the dashboard equivalent. It provides the framework for narrative paths to emerge and, consequently, a story can unfold if all the right pieces are in place. If business is normal, there is no story. However, as soon as there is an issue or some highlight, it will be clear and apparent what it is and what needs to be done to resolve it.

That sounds like a lot to expect from a dashboard. Fortunately, there is a formulaic way to get there. It is called scenario mapping, a means to take BVQs, determine their related visualizations and, most importantly, identify the actions that need to be taken should a set of criteria be met.

Understanding actions

An action, in the context of a dashboard, is something done or performed in response to an identified issue or highlight that will bring alignment and/or progress towards the stated goals of the dash-board. As is often the case, little thought is given to actions and contemplating what situations and scenarios would trigger such actions. Is it any wonder that adoption is low when so much is left to fate?

STORY

I was working on a dashboard for a retail product company. A large part of their business was ensuring retailers had enough inventory of their products, so they did not go out of stock. We created a chart on their dashboard that would map out current store inventory versus forecasted demand, by product and store. The title of that chart was: "Do we have enough inventory in stock at our stores based on the forecasted demand?" It was very easy to see on the chart, a bubble chart as it happens, which store/product combinations were at risk of running out of inventory in the short term. The question here was what to do with that information.

After some discussion and a couple of interviews, there were basically two actions that would typically be taken in such a scenario:

1   Someone would call the store in question and ask for their current inventory level for that product. There would be two possible answers to that. First, the inventory level is accurate and they need more or, second, their inventory reporting was incorrect, and they needed to update their inventory level.

2   In the case where the store needed more inventory, then the action needed to be taken to ship them more inventory, so their product levels were at an appropriate count.

With the typical workflow understood, the question was, who performs these actions? If that connection is not made then this was just going to be another dashboard that, while insightful, did not lead to a resolution. Following further conversations, there were up to three roles/individuals that needed to be involved in any combination of action for that specific question. Once they were identified, then a series of automated notifications could be sent to them, once the requisite conditions were met. This was then reflected on the dashboard that the notifications had been sent already and that a workflow was already underway to bring resolution.

This simple process saved hours of manual work every week. Over the course of a year, it equated to hundreds of hours saved. Yet spending the extra time during requirements gathering and design of the dashboard took approximately a week of additional effort in order to think through the various actions and scenarios. Quite the return on investment!

As much of the unknown as possible needs to be explored prior to building the dashboard. A significant reason that dashboards fail to be adopted is because they lack the business value and a return on investment (ROI). For the end user, are they getting an ROI for spending their time using a dashboard? Is the dashboard something they just look at or is it a vehicle for change and impact? If it is to be the latter, then time and effort must be spent upfront in understanding how that impact can be effected, what are the specific actions that are going to make such an impact, and under what set of conditions.

It sounds like a simple task, but the impact is significant. This is one of the largest differences between dashboards that get adopted and those that do not. It is an invisible gap in the insight creation process that must be addressed. For every BVQ, there need to be corresponding actions taken in order for the promise of "actionable insights" to be realized. The days of building insights in a silo and vacuum are gone with this approach. It demands collaboration, interaction, and discussion and it is why the process places an emphasis on people engagement.

The process of achieving this is through understanding scenarios and scenario mapping. Scenario mapping is the process of building stories with the available data, the practical process through which the narrative pathways are realized.

Scenario mapping

Scenario mapping is the process of taking a BVQ at one end and assigning the various scenarios that might impact the answer to that question at the other end. In between are several steps to break down the BVQ into a series of elements, including KPIs, charts, and filters. For an example of this in action, visit the book website.

With the value being in taking action and connecting that action to a BVQ, one is still left with the gap of how to visualize that in a dashboard. The visualization aspect can be especially challenging for anyone without data visualization expertise or, at least, they may perceive it as difficult, whether that is the case or not. Just like the simplicity of the questions approach was leveraged in defining the BVQs, a similar approach is needed for visualization. It must be abstracted from the perceived difficulty in picking the exact right chart.

Starting on the leftmost side is the BVQ. On the rightmost side is the set of conditions and actions to be taken. The glue in the middle is what will be used to design the visual layer of insight, the vehicle for impact, i.e., the dashboard. The first of these is "What does the end user need to see?" A natural language description of what the end user expects to be able to see to understand both the context and any impact for that specific BVQ. Next is to consider whether there is an associated KPI that is needed and, finally, how this question would need to be filtered.

What does the end user need to see?

A common disconnect in data visualization is what the user wants to see and what ends up being developed. People may already have their favorite way of looking at data, regardless of whether it is a best practice or not. On occasion, the preference can be so strong that not following it can become a barrier to adoption. To address that, gathering user input early is necessary and that is partly the rationale for working with the end user to establish their preference. Another reason is to increase partnership in the design stages, so the end user feels like they are playing a role in the design of their dashboard.

Typical responses can range from a very broad, non-technical, description all the way to defining the precise chart type and the exact axis that the user wants. It is deliberately a gray area in order to capture the wide range of expectations, preferences, and technical ability. The idea being that anyone can have a seat at the design table and have their opinion heard.

Often, there is a discussion and some back-and-forth at this stage, as well there should be. For this is the point where the end user must really start thinking about what they want and go through the mental process of envisioning the end state that will help them with their goals. There will be no surprises once the completed dashboard lies before them because they played a part in designing what it is going to look like.

Of note is that chart selection is not necessarily happening here. It might, if the user has a strong preference and provides a strong signal, but what is more likely is something along the lines of: "I want to see the historical trend of what inventory has been over the last few years." A more technical person might opine: "I want to see a trend line chart with a line for each of the past three years spanned across the monthly financial calendar." It does not mean there is not any room for applying data visualization best practices, but it does establish a starting point and foundational understanding on which to build. Plenty more on this to come, but this approach bridges user preference, where it exists, to data visualization in an accessible and approachable way for non-technical people.

Key performance indicators

A key performance indicator, or KPI, is a means of measuring how a company is progressing towards its stated objectives across a defined set of criteria or categories. At the inception of the process, the strategy template had an area for listing the desired objectives. Those objects should have informed the BVQs, and now each BVQ may need a means of tracking progress with KPIs. This is to ensure fidelity of the value chain and to maximize end user awareness that there is a clear purpose and vision behind the dashboard. It is the wider story of the dashboard, the journey to achieving the stated objectives.

To create a KPI, there are several factors to consider in making it both achievable and useful:

- Does it directly relate to the BVQ, which in turn is tied to the strategy?
- Can it be measured? Does the data support it?
- Can it be changed and influenced by action by the end user?
- Is it easy to understand?
- Can it be measured in an appropriate cadence for the dashboard, such as weekly, monthly, etc.?

There are whole books written about KPIs, their importance, and how to define them, and this is a field worthy of greater exploration. For the purposes of this process, creating KPIs aligned to the above criteria is more than sufficient. However, KPIs are not just created in isolation. It has taken several steps along the process to arrive at the KPI creation stage; the groundwork has already been laid for creating KPIs.

A KPI only becomes impactful if progress is made against it and, for that to happen, responsibility for it must be assigned. In this situation, it is the end user that is being assigned the responsibility to move that KPI. Otherwise, it may not be useful to have on their dashboard. If the end user does not have any agency to influence the KPI then they are less likely to care about it, or their interest in it may be short-lived once they notice that. There are cases where it is beneficial to have a KPI visible that goes beyond the influence of the end user in order to provide wider organizational context, but these should be kept to a minimum.

The KPI is to be the primary vehicle to measure change and progress. More importantly, it will be used to track the impact of actions that are taken. Did the actions taken from the dashboard last week make a measurable impact this week? Consider the KPI the pulse check to quickly assess impact and whether the taken actions are providing the desired resolution. If they are not, perhaps either the strategy needs to be revisited or the actions are not impactful. Either way, the feedback provides the opportunity to improve.

Subsequently, the velocity of the KPI is vital—how often can it be refreshed? If it is too slow then the end user feels it is disconnected and will likely log into the dashboard less, will take fewer actions, and progress towards the goals will be slowed. So careful consideration must be given to the user experience and maintenance of user engagement with the dashboard. Ideally, some excitement exists for the user to log in to see if their actions have had an impact. There is a degree of gamification potential to keep users coming back to track their progress.

A good KPI is not just a number in isolation. Like a good story, it requires context. How has it changed since last time, what is the trend, and how is it progressing towards its goal? These are the common questions that should be addressed with a KPI. Progress towards a goal is often stated as a percentage, though some will have a percentage and an absolute number, depending on what the context needed by the end user is. For example, an effective sales KPI might include the current revenue number, the revenue goal, and how the revenue has changed since last week.

The level of detail depends on the end user and what they care about. Not only that, but perhaps the KPI takes time for a change to be reflected, or there might be some other rationale for a delay in measuring impact. In such cases, it may be worth exploring subsets of the KPI and aspects that might change in a shorter amount of time. A slow-moving KPI may be more strategic in nature and not of sufficient granularity to be measurable over shorter periods, in which case it would need to be supplemented with more tactical KPIs.

Of course, there are many industry standard KPIs that can be researched and leveraged, and those should be the first port of call. For most situations, there will be industry standard KPIs already defined. In situations where standards are not applicable, then a little more effort needs to be spent on defining what they might be. For example, some typical KPIs include:

- net profit margin
- monthly recurring revenue
- net promoter score

- employee attrition rate
- cost of goods sold
- monthly new leads
- customer lifetime value
- cost per acquisition
- revenue growth rate

Not all BVQs will need a KPI, but just going through the exercise for each BVQ is a rich activity to have the end user participate in. It has a remarkable focusing effect on weeding out useless metrics and chart junk that can end up on dashboards. Not only that, they support aligning actions with the ability to measure the impact those actions will have on the KPI and the wider goals and objectives.

How should it be filtered?

For each BVQ, there may be several ways the end user may want to filter on it. This is not an invitation to just put all available filters on the table. Each filter must be considered on its own merits and how it supports the end user but also deepens the understanding of any narrative. Will adding this filter support taking an action? This is the question that must be asked. More filters mean more clicks on a dashboard. Too many filters can mean there is not a good enough understanding of the persona the dashboard is being designed for, or the persona is too broad and needs to be revisited.

Filters should not be added to mask poor design or to try to overcome a lack of proper requirements gathering. They can inadvertently be used as a Band Aid in an attempt to satisfy user needs. It is the equivalent of the trap in software development that adding more features to an interface is a good thing, versus focusing on simplicity and user experience. Filters can obfuscate a path to action. If the only means to determining an action is through filters, then it might suggest going back to the drawing board. Filters should add to and complement the story but not be a requirement for the narrative to function. The process puts greater emphasis on design and understanding the goals and behaviors of the end user persona. A positive and modern user experience minimizes clicks. The fewer the number of clicks to action, the better. Therefore, the aim is to minimize the number of filters on a dashboard.

The need for filters is sometimes confused with simply selecting the right chart type. A symptom of that can be a filter that only applies to a select few charts on a dashboard, i.e., it is a special case filter. Special cases mean bad design. There should be no special cases. The first port of call for a filter special case is to explore whether it can be solved with a chart. For a filter to be appropriate, it must satisfy several criteria:

- The filter must apply to all visual elements on a dashboard.
- It cannot be addressed with a chart or KPI.
- It should support deeper context and understanding.

Typical filters include time, geography, and various categorical types. It can almost be an unconscious decision to just include these standard filters on every tab in a dashboard. However, they may add little value. The ideal way to start is with no filters and this challenges you to design with a minimal number of clicks until filters become the only available route to unlock certain insights.

Scenarios for taking action

For each BVQ there should be at least one scenario for which action needs to be taken. If there is no scenario, then why is it there? Unless there is an abundance of rationale for why it should be present without any scenarios for action, then consider dropping it. As an example, a scenario for the BVQ "Do our stores have enough inventory for the next month of forecasted sales?", here are some scenarios where action would need to be taken:

- if there is not enough inventory
- if a stock check has not been conducted
- if the stock data has not been refreshed

Determining these scenarios first makes it easier for the end user to determine the workflows and actions that may be required to address the scenarios and bring resolution to them. There is also the added benefit of exploring opportunities for automation of tasks and notifications. If a scenario is triggered, is it 100 percent necessary to only discover that by having to log into the dashboard? Could a notification be sent or a process triggered to flag the issue right away?

It also enables more efficient design and groupings of visual elements on a dashboard. By understanding the scenarios for action, there may be other supporting data that is needed to get further context. With such a degree of focus, the path to action can be shortened.

Actions

Coming full circle, and the entire purpose for having a dashboard is the fulfillment of the actions. The actions must be aligned to a specific scenario. It must have sufficient nuance to be easily executed by the end user or, at least, for the end user to know what needs to be done, whether they are the one taking the action or assigning it to someone else. A pitfall to avoid is actions that are too general. It is akin to kicking the can down the road and expecting to figure it out later. The destination of that road is low adoption and a lack of return on investment. Low adoption is very hard to pinpoint in retrospect. There can be a wide range of causes but principal amongst them is the inability to drive behavioral change.

Every BVQ should have at least one scenario for where action is needed, and every scenario needs at least one action. There may be several actions for a given scenario. To continue the inventory example, taking the scenario "If there is not enough inventory", here are some example actions that could be applicable:

- Call the affected store and ask whether their inventory levels are up to date, request an update if not and recheck whether the inventory level is still a concern. If it is then proceed to the next action.
- Fulfill a new order of the affected product to the impacted store.

This example describes two actions for a given scenario. Taking those actions should ultimately resolve the problem that was identified. Since they are tied to a scenario which, in turn, is tied to a business value question, then those actions are aligned towards a strategic goal. Therefore, the end user is executing the vision for the organization, and fidelity to the value chain of insight is maintained.

Actions can fall into several categories, ranging from phone calls and emails to notifications and triggering automated workflows. Of course, the more effort an action takes, the less likely it is to be completed. Therefore, the opportunity at this point of the process is to explore how to reduce the friction in executing an action. This may further open the door to improvements in organizational process, workflows, and the regular way of doing business. Just defining actions does not mean the end user will execute them.

STORY

In the early days of working on understanding and experimenting how to make it easy for users to execute actions that are highlighted on a dashboard, it seemed like an obvious opportunity to see how an action could be triggered directly from the dashboard itself. The idea was that people were less likely to take the action in situations where it was too much manual effort and hassle, even though the action itself might be trivial to execute. The idea was to make it very easy for the user to make it happen.

A very common action was to export a specific chart to a CSV so it could be emailed to a colleague. Another was to call so-and-so and have a conversation about the issue. A real go-to was to schedule a meeting to discuss the contents of the dashboard. As I was to learn, these were faux actions. The phone calls did not happen. The meeting invites were never sent. People were basically putting off dealing with taking the necessary action.

What I noticed was that I was skimming over the step of assigning actions to questions. It was a lot of effort to engage the right stakeholders and determine what actions their subordinates could and should be able to execute versus just setting meetings and having chats that rarely led to anything much changing. Agency to act and accountability had to come as part of an organization's data culture. If people were being armed with data to make better decisions with, but there was not a corresponding shift in the operating model, then there was still going to be a bottleneck.

Of course, that kind of approach is far broader than building dashboards. It resonates throughout the entire organization to its very foundations. Through research and some hard lessons learned, I understood that companies that successfully leveraged data but also made the shift to be agile enough to execute on the information in the data were the ones that were transforming their market and their sales. They were the ones that were rapidly adjusting to changing market conditions and, rather than shrinking, experienced rapid growth when the economy was bumpy.

The journey further emphasized for me the importance of change management but also the layers of stories that went far reaching, beyond the comparatively simple activity of creating insights in a dashboard. It gave me an entirely new perspective when starting a new project about what was needed for it to deliver on the promise of BI and analytics.

The scenario mapping flow

With an appreciation for each of the elements of the scenario map, how they come together and work together is next. But first, a quick recap of the journey to date. The project started with defining the goals and objectives, leveraging the strategy template. Several interviews were conducted to establish and define the end user personas. Following that, the BVQs were itemized and vetted against the available data, which resulted in a prioritized list of BVQs for the current iteration. Now, each BVQ will have the scenario mapping treatment that includes:

1 The BVQ itself

2 What the end user needs to see to answer that BVQ

3 Are KPIs required for the BVQ?

4 What filters, if any, support the answer?

5 The scenarios or conditions that action might be warranted

6 The actions that are to be taken for each scenario

Equating the above steps to the three-act narrative structure, it would break down like this:

- Act 1 is the content of the dashboard:
  - the BVQs
  - the KPIs
  - what the user needs to see (i.e., the charts)
  - the filters
- Act 2 is the highlight in the dashboard:
  - the scenarios or conditions—if one is triggered then the user can see it
- Act 3 is the call to action:
  - the action(s) to take based on the scenario

This is the format for how storytelling will emerge with this process. It provides the path for the story to happen but does not guarantee there will be a story every time the dashboard is opened. That depends on what is going on with the business on any given day. However, based on the chosen BVQs and scenarios, if there is a story there, it will be told.

Even if a BVQ lacks value or importance, that will be surfaced with this exercise. The BVQs that do not have an action are candidates for review to see if they should be included or not. Another issue might be that there are so many BVQs that it takes a very long time to go through them all. In such cases, it would be beneficial to limit the number per iteration. Instead, focus on quick wins versus trying to solve too much in one iteration—spread them out over time.

This is a comprehensive way to connect business strategy to a visualization that tactically drives change in alignment to the strategy in a way that engages the end user. It can take time and effort, above and beyond just jumping into development, but the rewards are worth it. The time invested here translates to ROI later. With experience, it becomes faster and more efficient to the point that it is indispensable and almost inconceivable to skip over!

In practical application, the process can be facilitated in several ways. A low-tech and efficient way is to use sticky notes, either real or on a virtual whiteboard. By using sticky notes, it remains accessible and less likely to be perceived as beyond anyone's abilities to understand. Sticky notes are a great equalizer for technical ability. In the example below, the first sticky note is a BVQ. Beyond that are each of the steps to bring that BVQ to reality by adding the various inputs and ending in the action or actions related to it. Keep in mind there can be one too many relationships between a BVQ and both scenarios and actions.

Getting to the "So what?"

Telling stories with data is achievable, and in this chapter the vehicle for doing that is to leverage scenario mapping. It may differ from other expectations of what storytelling with data is but it is practical and applicable to the real world, especially for those who lack the confidence with storytelling. This is all achieved through the scenario mapping approach.

A completed scenario map is no small thing. However, taking the time to do it makes life considerably easier at the next stages. The scenario maps have brought the end users and stakeholders several steps closer to making impact in the organization. While little has happened in terms of building a dashboard so far, much has happened in building the framework for adoption and addressing the common causes of low adoption by building out the various narrative pathways.

Arriving at this point is what few organizations achieve successfully when building insight, because it is hard! If solving adoption was easy, then there would not be the data culture issues that many organizations currently face. The problems of adoption do not magically disappear. What the process has done is take the issues that surface at the end of a typical project, move them earlier in the journey, and provide a framework for addressing them.

So, buckle up, because the next steps in the process are starting to apply visuals to the scenarios! This is where it all starts to take shape and the fruits of the process are to be visualized. In the next chapter the goal is to take all of this hard work and visualize it in a rapid and structured way so the narrative pathways that have been created here can be represented on the dashboard.

08

Crafting the vision

Before starting my career in analytics, I was a director of UI/UX for a mobile software application company in Singapore. I had a small team of UI designers and the UX aspects of the group were largely left to me as that skill was not filled in the team. We had to manage a consistent user experience across both the desktop web interfaces through to the mobile experiences, both mobile web and through our mobile application.

This was in the early days of mobile UX and there was not an abundance of frameworks and libraries available, so a lot of testing was needed. We had a bank of various phones available for testing out across the wide range of resolutions. It generally entailed adapting the design to at least six resolutions so that we were addressing about 90 percent of user devices. That last 10 percent of devices would take far too much effort for my small team to tackle.

In any given month there were new devices coming out by the flagship phone manufacturers and we would have to stay on top of those. It was a lot of work just managing the scaling of fonts, resolution-specific images, and resizing of buttons. All this work that goes into the interface that the end user does not really see. They only notice it if it is poorly executed. And if they find something, it may break their experience and drive them away from it and, ultimately, impact their adoption of the tool. Even with the greatest software, the judgment lies in the experience of the interface. I learned that lesson the hard way.

Much has changed and evolved since the early human–computer interfaces of the 1970s and 1980s. User interface design has evolved from a text-based experience to context-rich, task-oriented experiences. Not only that, the technical capabilities driving those interfaces have greatly changed as well as where that experience happens. They used to be via big mainframe computers with green and black terminal interfaces. Now they can be on devices as small and portable as watches. The field of human–computer interaction has never had it so good, and it is only getting better.

While it is the software startups and enterprises that have primarily driven this innovation, the progress eventually makes its way over to the interfaces for data, BI, and analytics. So much so that the modern BI platforms have compelling UI capabilities with considerable opportunity to customize and tailor the end user experience. A number of the platforms now support mobile experiences without the need to design specifically for those varying screen sizes.

Life has become easier for creating dashboards, allowing people to focus more on how to deliver insight versus getting into the weeds of how to render the experience across a range of devices, among many other challenges. Crafting the visuals for a dashboard is where the worlds of data visualization, user interface (UI) design, and user experience all intersect. It can be an immensely fun and rewarding part of the process as it provides the first tangible glimpses of what the product, a dashboard in this case, is going to look like. UI design is typically accompanied by the creation of "mock-ups" or wireframes of the design to get user feedback and this chapter is going to dive into the process of designing and wireframing dashboards.

There is very little new under the sun and that is true for adapting and applying UI design principles for a dashboard. Since a dashboard is fundamentally a user interface, the best practices for interface design still apply, though there are some additional ones that are specific to dashboards.

With that in mind, and before diving into the intricacies of dashboard design, there are a few core principles to understand in the realm of user interface best practices.

User interface design principles

The user UI is naturally a vital part of any software or data product. The ideal interface is one that users hardly even notice. It is seamless and intuitive, like an extension of their being. However, an imperfect interface can be a barrier to users and they might not be able to get beyond the bad user experience, no matter how good the underlying system is. To maximize the potential for a good experience, there are principles that can be followed to help the would-be interface designer be successful. Over the years, the list of principles has become extensive but here are the most important ones, particularly as they pertain to dashboards.

Focus on clarity

The purpose of the dashboard should be clear to the persona it is designed for. They should understand why it is important and how it can help them. The interface should be intuitive enough that they know what to expect and how it will function when they interact with it. Clarity supports adoption, confusion drives adoption further. This applies to all the visual elements, from the tabs on the dashboards to the tooltips.

Consistent structure

Keeping a consistent visual structure breeds familiarity and trust in an interface. Users will start to feel at home when they know what to expect from the layout. Structure includes where the navigation is, placements of KPIs, filters, and charts as well as the use of color, font, and visual ordering such as a grid system.

Minimize distraction

The visual elements of an interface should all be in service of action, of supporting the user in what they need to do. There should be no visual element screaming for attention if it does not serve the purpose of the interface. People's time is precious, and, in the enterprise, there are typically so many things competing for that attention. Minimizing distractions allows the task at hand to be completed faster and more efficiently.

Minimal interface

It almost sounds like an oxymoron, but the less interface the better. Indeed, the ideal interface is the one that does not exist as the user can directly manipulate reality with their hands. Obviously that is not feasible with data and information, but the fewer layers to the interface the better. This means limiting the use of UI elements as much as possible. So, the user spends their time on what is important instead of fiddling around with flashy buttons, sliders, animations, and other visual flair. The goal is to design an interface that is as close to direct manipulation as it can be, so the user feels like they are manipulating it with their hands.

Feedback

An interface should be responsive to user inputs and provide a feedback loop to user interaction, when and where appropriate. If a filter is clicked, then it should visually indicate it has been clicked and remain selected until the filter is deselected. When hovering over an element in a chart, a tooltip could pop up offering further detail. It should be fast and efficient so that the current state of the interface is quickly understood.

Accessibility

Further to the UX aspects of accessibility in Chapter 3, the best interfaces are designed so all users can interact with them. The modern BI tools are already addressing aspects of this, such as appropriate use of colors for those who have a related visual impairment, as well as high-contrast features built directly into the tool.

Minimize steps to action

In typical software interfaces, the aim is to have a single CTA, or call to action. One thing that the user is directed to do. The more actions, the higher the likelihood the user becomes confused by the interface. This requires themes to be consistent for any view of an interface and to not have competing objectives. For a dashboard, a tab would be focused on a single topic, such as inventory levels. It would not be ideal to focus on inventory levels and employee turnover, for example, where there are very different actions that would be required based on the scenarios. Where action is needed, the fewer steps the user must take the better. Minimizing the number of clicks to action helps the user be more effective.

Appearance matches behavior

People generally have an expectation of how things behave. If something has wings, it probably flies. If a tool has a power button it probably turns it on. With interfaces, visual elements should behave like how they look. Meaning, just by looking at a UI element, the user knows what it will do. Clicking a filter will update the view with that selection. It needs to look like it is a filter. Likewise, a navigation button would need to look and act like the user would expect. It looks like it will navigate the user to another tab and, when clicked, it does exactly that. Another common term for this is "form follows function." This must also be applied with consistency. A button should not look the same as a filter, because they behave differently. A navigation tab element should not be mistaken for tooltip action.

Visual hierarchy

A visual hierarchy helps the user understand what is most important in the structure of an interface. A clear hierarchy is when the user can see a viewing order and where their attention is being directed to, in a defined sequence. A poorly designed visual hierarchy leaves the user wondering where they should be looking. Such interfaces might be overly cluttered and be lacking a purpose. If the interface lacks a structure, then the user will be challenged in arriving at what action to take and, ultimately, adoption suffers. By applying a strong hierarchy, it becomes easier to direct the user's attention to what matters and what they need to do about it.

Organization

Modern interfaces seek to group similar elements together where a relationship is indicated by placement. The user must think less about how things work or how elements are related. If there is any question of the user having to figure something out, then one possibility is that it may not be organized optimally. Ultimately, it comes down to keeping things simple.

Inline help

Of course, the best interface does not need any support or help in how to interact with it. But that can often be unrealistic, especially when a tool or BI platform is being exposed to a user for the first time. This can also be the case for a new report or dashboard. Regardless, supporting the user when and where they are, with the appropriate context, is a trait of an excellent interface. However, it should generally only be available when needed and not be seen persistently, as that might frustrate experienced users. There is much more on this in later chapters, as it is a key ingredient to adoption.

Building on principles

Sticking to these principles will already make for a compelling dashboard experience. However, to truly drive adoption, there are specific applications of the principles that must be tailored for data and insight applications. Dashboards have several unique properties that necessitate this. They are often dynamic in nature; they change from day to day or even minute to minute. They need to drive action, often with several scenarios that need to be catered to. Finally, those actions need to be tracked in some way so that the impact can be attributed back to the action itself.

Believe it or not, much of the hard work has already been done, as it should be before making any attempt to visualize the end product. The stage is now set to build on the scenario mapping stage and start crafting what the dashboard is going to look like, to determine the specific layout, charts, colors, fonts, and other visual elements. While there are many layout options available, simplicity and consistency will rule the day and only the layouts with the widest applicability are going to be explored. That is not to say that other layouts lack merit. For specific personas and use cases, they may well be preferable over the more broadly applicable layouts.

STORY

When I am speaking on data visualization and dashboard layouts in conferences, a common question that I am asked is where to place the filters. Should they be on the right or on the left? People usually end up taking sides based on the BI platform they are using and the default placement of filters within their chosen technology. Honestly, I find it as good a reason as any to have a preference for where to place filters.

Certainly, there is some research to indicate the ideal placement of filters. However, I am yet to encounter a situation where filter placement has been the most significant barrier to adoption. If that is flagged as a big problem then, in my mind, it is time for celebration because it means much larger adoption challenges have been overcome, to such a degree that filter placement is the most significant problem to tackle.

More important than the exact place to put filters on a dashboard is being consistent about the placement and how it supports both the context and actions the dashboard is driving towards. So, whether they are on the right, the left, the top is somewhat secondary to how they support the user to achieve their intended goals.

Dashboard layout types

Outside of data exploration, there are three main types of dashboards to consider: strategic, operational, and tactical. Each one of these tends to have different objectives and end user personas. Strategic dashboards are more focused on high-level stories and tracking against KPIs over broad periods of time. Operational dashboards are often at a management level where a faster cadence is necessary and may get more into certain details. Tactical dashboards focus more on doing and taking action over shorter periods of time.

In general, there are variations to the optimal layouts for each of these dashboard types but there is significant overlap between them also. The more strategic a dashboard, the more focus it would have on KPIs and less clicking to get to insight is preferred. So, the layout of the dashboard would put a weighting towards KPIs and place less emphasis on larger format charts. Contrast this with more tactical dashboards where a bias is given towards charts being able to diagnose specific issues and take the according action with them. Operational dashboards fall somewhere in the middle. Since the bulk of dashboards fall into being operational or tactical, that is the primary layout to cater to.

Dashboard hierarchy

A hierarchy ranks the importance of the visual elements of an interface. What are the most important elements to draw users' attention to? Taking a deliberate approach to the hierarchy allows the designer to better address the needs of the end user and to reduce confusion and frustration. The major UI elements of a dashboard are the KPIs, charts, filters, title, and navigation. With some exceptions, they can generally be ranked thus:

1 KPIs
2 Charts
3 Filters

4 Tab navigation

5 Dashboard title

KPIs take the top spot because they are the visual inflection point between business strategy and taking action. They should be prominent and, if attention is needed, the user's attention is quickly directed there. Consider the busy manager who only has a few seconds to spare. Their attention is limited. They don't need additional cognitive load placed on them to figure out what they need to do. The KPI is how to reel their attention and focus into an action funnel.

Charts take the second place as they are the visual element that adds context to the KPIs but also directs the path to action. The attention of the user goes from the KPI, if something has called their attention, to the chart, to understand the why for what is going on with that KPI. The chart can add context in several ways, from the details within the chart itself to supplementary information such as tooltips and the ability to drill down when needed.

Filters play a supportive role for a well-designed dashboard, not a primary one. For interfaces that are designed for several personas filters might have more prominence, as filtering may be the first action a user might need to take in order to reduce the noise that is present for other personas. It's not a bad thing necessarily, as often the reality is that there is neither the time nor resources to narrow the focus to one persona. The user experience does indeed suffer unless the filters can be applied by default based on the role of the user. Recall that filters are sometimes used as a bandage to mask poor requirements gathering. A reason why filter placement is considered important, and some people spend a disproportionate amount of time worrying about it, is because the filter is trying to do a lot—it has been given an unfair responsibility to apply a crutch to bad design.

Tab navigation is the vehicle for the user to move between tabs on the dashboard. It can be an afterthought and almost left entirely to the whims of the BI platform being used, i.e., however the platform places and deals with tabs. Some platforms do this moderately well, others do it so poorly that it can be hard to find, and the user might assume there is only one tab or may not appreciate that tabs exist at all.

There are several navigational experiences most people are already familiar with that can be mimicked. First, web browsers make extensive use of tabbed navigation and it has almost become a natural and ingrained user experience for anyone accessing the internet. Second, the navigation on many websites uses a menu navigation structure that would be in a similar way to tabs. While the navigation does not need to take center stage, it must be clear enough that it is there and there is no ambiguity as to what it does. The closer it comes to a familiar experience, the better in this case.

The specific placement of the above visual elements depends on a few criteria and the hierarchy does not necessarily imply that an element higher up in the hierarchy is placed higher visually on the interface. It means it would be more prominent in drawing the user's attention. There are a few considerations to adoption if it is the first iteration of a new dashboard and there is concern about how the users will adapt to the new interface. In such cases, consideration might be given to emphasizing the title and navigation.

Tabs and grouping of BVQs

Many users, if not all, are already familiar with the concept and functionality of tabs. What may be less evident, however, is how to naturally structure and name the tabs so they seem intuitive and natural to the user. It is a vital step as the grouping will determine how the narrative plays out on a specific tab. There can be a little trial and error necessary to get it all dialed in, but a safe place to start is grouping the BVQs and their associated outputs from scenario mapping by topic and theme. Chances are, there might be a relationship between some of the BVQs.

It is often the case that the various options for themes are already established. In the case of a human resources dashboard, the tabs to initially explore are categories that most HR professionals are already very familiar with, such as attrition, retention, recruiting, composition, etc. Since they are already established topics that the user is comfortable with, they are a natural place to start for grouping questions and naming the tabs.

With experience, it becomes easier to anticipate which questions should be answered together on the same tab. Which questions have some overlap, or which ones are subsets of the same broader questions? Consider how the questions should interact with each other and whether there would be benefit to seeing the answer to one question in the context of another. Should that relationship not be evident, and there might be no relationship, another way to group is by questions that have the same filters, as the filters can be a by-product of similarity and relationship.

Outside of the individual tabs for answering specific questions, there is occasionally the need for some form of overview or summary tab. A tab that distills all the other tabs and gives a snapshot of the entire dashboard. This is especially true in situations where a dashboard has many tabs and there is just too much to take in or too many clicks are needed to get through all the tabs. It is a table of contents with the key points for what is the state of the dashboard.

However, before building the summary tab, all the other tabs should be assembled first to understand how each tab is structured and how many tabs will be needed. The summary tab can distract from the overall purpose of driving action, as a summary tab may not directly drive action. The summary tab can also be a useful way of scaling the dashboard to multiple, but aligned, end users. For example, a human resources professional might leverage the majority of the tabs, but an HR manager might just look for the high level of what is going on and view the summary tab. This maintains alignment between the goals and objectives of the dashboard and across the HR chain of command, in this example. The summary tab should not display information that is not available on other tabs, but it could give a more suitable visualization for that information that can be digested at a higher level.

One approach for a summary tab is to have a visual for each of the tabs that gives an insight into what is happening in that tab and if the user needs to dive into it to take any action. This is especially important where there are many tabs and clicking through each tab is not a viable option. In such cases, a summary tab can increase adoption and usage of the dashboard by making the user experience more targeted. Paradoxically, the less time spent in the dashboard may increase adoption, so long as the reason for the shorter engagement is good user experience and not someone unable to fulfill their needs with the interface, or it becomes a frustrating experience.

In later chapters there will be further discussion about the summary tabs as well as additional tabs that support adoption, enablement, and training.

One dashboard layout to rule them all

Simplicity is king. Having a go-to dashboard layout to use in most situations reduces the time it takes to ramp up a new project. It provides a starting point that can be tweaked and tailored as needed but, just by itself, will be acceptable for most situations without needing to be touched at all. With the visual hierarchy established, the next step is to determine how to render it in a layout. This layout, the primary layout, for a dashboard is well positioned for operational and tactical dashboards. A change to this layout may be necessary for strategic dashboards but that will be dealt with later in this chapter.

Tying this back to the narrative structure, Act 1 is the title, navigation, and the filters, Act 2 is surfaced through the KPIs, and Act 3 is realized through the charts, by and large. Represented in this manner, most of the screen real estate is dedicated to taking action and resolution. It gradually scales. Several examples are available for download on the book website.

Act 1 content familiarizes the user with the interface, what it is about, and how it works. This content should take the least amount of screen real estate, where possible. Failing that, it should be the lowest in the visual hierarchy, the least attention grabbing.

Act 2 content occupies a little more space and is placed in a prominent location on the interface. In contrast to the Act 1 content, Act 2 should rank the highest on the visual hierarchy and should be the first thing a user's attention is drawn to. What does that mean? KPIs should be large, bold, and impossible to miss if one of them is screaming for attention.

In this layout, the largest area is dedicated to the charts. It does not infer highest importance, more that additional space may be needed in order to understand why a KPI might be off and to gain the necessary context. While they are second in the visual hierarchy, a seasoned user might just go straight to the charts and skip over the KPIs if they know what they are looking for.

The narrative mostly unfolds from top to bottom, with the title and navigation setting the context, the KPIs below those determining whether something needs attention and, below that, the action that needs to be taken. Before breaking down the primary layout into specific visual elements, there are some other layouts that should be considered from the conceptual level.

Alternative layouts

Before breaking down the primary layout further, it is worth exploring other layouts from the three-act perspective. Where the primary layout takes a holistic approach to a view, it can be more suitable to have a clear and direct path and connection from one KPI to one or more charts that have a linear visual connection. To maintain that connectivity, the KPI and charts would be visually aligned. This is the confined narrative layout, where the subject matter and content are very well understood and have a limited number of factors that influence the story.

It can be very easy to structure and design this way and, possibly, could be a more appropriate starting template for an organization. The narrative structure can be a little confusing initially, as it happens from the title and navigation and then eye tracks with the KPIs downwards but to the left side, and moves from there to the right, per KPI. However, once established, it creates a compelling way to think about the drivers for each KPI, assuming sufficient context and action can be imparted by the limited number of charts that can be aligned to each KPI.

It does present a different design challenge than the primary layout. With the primary layout, a wider narrative can exist with cross-connectivity with all the KPIs and charts in the view. In this layout, however, it can be more restricted to the narrative between and individual KPI being tied to individual charts. Again, not necessarily a bad thing, but applicable to more nuanced use cases that require a little more thought than the primary layout.

Another layout to consider is for the strategic type of scenario discussed earlier in the chapter. Strategic dashboards focus more on the executive type of persona where they will not be the ones executing the actions from a dashboard and would have others take the action. They fit the bill of "Who do I need to shout at?" versus "What do I need to do?" For this type of dashboard, more emphasis is placed on KPIs and less space is given to both filters and charts. Ideally, the executive would not have to click at all. This type of interface gives a pulse of the business with the Act 3 portion being fulfilled through meetings, calls, and actions outside of the interface.

STORY

As was customary, during the third year of my computer science degree, there was a six-month work placement. Most of my peers were planning on getting experience with some of the more established, and local, organizations such as Intel and Motorola. Most of them found roles in Cork, a few went to Dublin, and fewer still went further afield such as the UK. Possibly one of them ended up in Australia but I am a little foggy on that.

For me, I wanted to go somewhere I thought would be more exciting, in a field I was passionate about. Virtual reality (VR) was all the rage back then and there were not many places in Ireland one could get experience in it. I had to cast my eyes abroad. To Honolulu, to be precise. The company was a small VR simulation company that used the Unreal game engine as the basis for the interface.

My role was working on the "Briefing Module," basically a 2D interface where the player would set up their VR experience before putting on their VR headset. I was to do development using Macromedia's Lingo scripting language in Director, a long-since defunct and more powerful type of Flash. It is worth mentioning it was an unpaid internship and I was being put up in my boss's house along with a few other interns (who were getting paid).

Part of the challenge was that I did not know Lingo script yet, let alone be able to focus on the UI design! In my first week, I worked 104 hours so I could both get up to speed on what I needed to do but to also learn the Lingo scripting language. The second week got better at 96 hours with 80 becoming the norm a few weeks in.

Since Director could create interfaces in both 2D and 3D, I assumed 3D would be better. Why would it not, it has a whole extra dimension to work with! Without knowing it, I was dipping my toes into the world of data visualization for the first time. I started to find that people found the 2D interface faster and more intuitive than the 3D version. Even though the 3D was way cooler looking. I got my first taste of the importance of simplicity over visual complexity and how optimal 2D is for user interface design. The simplicity of the 2D interaction was both faster and preferred by the majority of users over the high-fashion 3D one.

Even to this day, with all the advances in graphical capability, 3D and VR are still rather niche, with the ideal application being around military simulations, high-risk training environments, and other non-consumer application.

The primary layout

Diving a little deeper into the primary layout, it places the title and navigation at the top of the dashboard, much like a website would. Positioned prominently under those are the KPIs, with the charts below them. In this layout, the filters are placed on the left and the navigation at the top, along with the title. To a degree, the chart titles also provide context and fulfill aspects of Act 1 content as well as opening the door for Act 3.

One of the principles of good interface design is to leverage a grid structure and that is evident in this layout. The grid makes alignment of the visual elements easier for the designer to position as well as creating a predictable sense of comfort and trust for the user.

The specific number of KPIs and charts varies, but this layout is a solid starting point. Variations in the number of KPIs range from three to six. Going beyond those may need the design to be reconsidered, possibly more or fewer tabs and a different grouping of the BVQs. The same goes for the number of charts—there can be some variation from one to up to six, depending on the situation and interaction between the charts.

Part of the rationale for having a range of KPIs of between three and six is the aesthetic composition of the interface. Too few and it may appear sparse and incomplete, almost like it is not ready for prime time. There are exceptions but, as a rule of thumb, it is better to reconsider the design if the number of KPIs on a tab drops below three. An excessive number of KPIs, seven or more, may lead to an overly cluttered interface and it can be harder for the user to focus on what needs attention. So, the three to six range is a comfortable target to have for KPIs, to know things are on the right track.

There are occasions when filters can occupy a lot of space. This can be common when a range of dates and time spans is desired, especially in financial analysis. It is not that these should necessarily be reduced, but they should be challenged from a design perspective. For example, is it necessary to have date filters by quarter, by month, by week, by day, as well as having a calendar filter? Some of this need might be satisfied by a mix of KPI design and chart design to reduce the number of filters needed.

The narrative for the primary layout, and others, has already been greatly accelerated through the scenario mapping process. How the narrative unfolds on the dashboard is a function of how the BVQs were grouped and the breakdown of each BVQ from scenario mapping.

With reference to the store inventory example, imagine how an inventory shortage could be highlighted, understood, be acted upon, and a resolution found. The KPI "Inventory at risk" is 3, meaning there are three products at risk of running out of inventory. There is a supporting KPI that is also showing an issue, "Revenue at risk." Just by looking at the KPIs, the user can already understand that there are three products with an inventory problem and the potential impact is $7.3 million. This is what the top layer of the interface should do; tell the user there is a problem, the magnitude of the problem, and where they should focus their attention.

Additional context is provided by the supporting charts. Without considering optimal chart selection, a natural language title above each chart indicates which charts would support the understanding of the KPIs above. A chart titled "Which products are likely to run out of stock in the next 30 days?" shows three outliers that are clearly visible. Moving the cursor over them reveals what products they are and some important additional details such as the impacted stores, the quantities and additional information that supports taking action.

Wireframes

A wireframe serves the purpose of getting feedback from the end user early and often. They are not connected to data. Their level of detail can range from being basic, low-fidelity, sketches on a whiteboard to incredibly high-fidelity representations of the dashboard that show animations and interactions for how the interface will behave. Most often, a level of detail somewhere in between is the optimal state for a wireframe.

There are many benefits to wireframing, and it should become an integral part of any data project that involves a user interface. When considering the costs that have been involved in surfacing insights in an organization, and the impact that a wireframe has versus the low level of effort it requires, it has a high return for influencing adoption.

The closer the wireframe approximates the desired end state, the better. However, there are trade-offs to be aware of. Spending too much time on creating wireframes can defeat the purpose of being quick and agile. It should not become a burden, and a definite preference is given to only being as detailed with the wireframe as needed in order for the audience to understand the vision and how it is going to look, directionally.

A happy medium for detail is enough quality to adequately describe what the visual elements are, while abstracting how it will exactly look in the technology the dashboard is ultimately going to be developed in. Of course, if there are considerable differences in layout between the wireframe and limitations in the technology that cannot support the wireframe, some accommodations must be made. The reason being is that the user might start expecting a certain layout, based on the wireframes, and it looks entirely different once it is developed. Some balance is needed in order to moderate expectations.

Another reason to not go the high-fidelity route with wireframes is to suspend the belief that they are connected to any kind of data source. Sketches on a whiteboard are clearly understood to not be connected to data. However, the closer the wireframes move to higher fidelity, the more they look like a real dashboard. When displaying the wireframes to the audience, they might think they are connected to data and that would raise the unnecessary discussion whether the numbers are right and why is such a number so far off, etc. It can attach negativity to wireframes, and the process in general, when expectations are not appropriately set.

Even when there is a strong argument for high-fidelity wireframes over lower fidelity, it is preferable to give a weighting to the low-fidelity option. Perhaps surprisingly, damage to adoption can easily happen here with audiences that are skeptical about change and new ways of representing data, and any reason or excuse that can be jumped on to cast it in a negative light are opportunities to avoid.

Saying all that, there are good reasons to use high-fidelity wireframes. When the end users clearly understand that they are wireframes, and there is no doubt that they are just mock-ups, then they have no expectation that the numbers should be accurate. Conversely, the wireframes could be created so that they do have an accurate reflection of the data. While still not connected to a data source of course, the wireframes could be designed with recent numbers that the audience is already familiar with, so it matches their expectations. Another case for high-fidelity wireframes is when the audience has been through the process several times and they know what to expect. A degree of change management has already happened, and they have some comfort and familiarity with the process.

The risk with wireframes really comes from people who have never been exposed to them and what they entail. With that knowledge gap, they then incorrectly, though understandably, apply what knowledge and mental model they do have about dashboards to the wireframe. It should be interactive, it should have real data, it should behave like a dashboard! However, none of those expectations is there for sketches on a whiteboard because a model and expectations already exist for what a whiteboard is capable of. It is very obviously not going to behave like a dashboard should and is merely a basic representation of one. The same can be said for sticky notes or any tactile and physical asset.

STORY

With wireframing being such a powerful tool, I am convinced that anyone in the business of building interfaces should always wireframe first before any development happens. To that end, I created the Dashboard Wireframe Kit. It is a very simply way to wireframe specifically for dashboards that has the benefits of clearly not being perceived as connected to data but the upside of having a wide range of charts that the users can see and pick from.

Over the years of working in data visualization, I started to notice that best practice is not always what the books say on the ideal chart selection. If the user can be involved in the selection of charts, it needs to be fast and agile. With the Kit they can quickly flick through the various chart options and see how they relate to answering each question. This then opens a discussion on how the charts can help them and why which chart options are better or worse for their needs.

On one project, with a very fast iteration cycle, the client wanted to quickly explore some alternative design options for an executive dashboard that was about to be released. We cracked open the Dashboard Wireframe Kit and, within ten minutes of working on a table in a corridor, designed an alternative tab on the dashboard that would better cater to a subset of the executives. The client found this to be a profoundly fast way to design and rapidly create requirements. He took a picture of the wireframe and just emailed it to his dashboard developers and, two hours later, they had developed the tab for what they saw in the picture.

In a pinch, a good wireframe is a distillation of the requirements and will have enough detail for a developer to look at, understand, and interpret what they need to do. From a developer's perspective, the higher fidelity a wireframe is the better, so less interpretation and guess work is needed to properly build the dashboard in the chosen platform. If they can see the chart types, the additional details surrounding a KPI, and the same filters, they can spend more time developing and less time asking questions and getting meetings on the books to align.

For those reasons, high-fidelity wireframes are better for developers, low-fidelity wireframes are better for the end users. That is not always the case, but they are good general rules to follow in the absence of experience. Does that mean that high-fidelity wireframes are always needed before handing off for development? Not at all! However, it does illustrate when to use one over the other. More often than not, if the steps of the process have been followed and there are the associated artifacts created accordingly, then low-fidelity wireframes are sufficient for both the end users and the engineers and BI developers.

It is certainly not a one-size-fits-all, however. For a certain organization, maybe high-fidelity wireframes are vital. An obvious difference is that the low fidelity could be implemented on almost any modern BI platform, whereas the high-fidelity wireframe must be tailored to a specific BI platform with alignment with the features and capabilities of that technology. Low-fidelity wireframes are intentionally lacking in quality and keep the focus on the overall layout and questions being answered.

Wireframes are the next logical extension of the scenario mapping process; it is a continuation rather than a net new activity. The wireframe adds visual details to the outputs of the scenario mapping work. For example, the KPIs are already established, but the wireframe indicates where they will be positioned in the layout, how big they will be and, if there are any other visual elements added to the KPI such as a target, percentage of change over time, absolute change of value, etc.

A wireframe version of the filter would show some of the items that can be filtered on. For example, if the filter is "Department" then the wireframe would show that as the title for the filter but also list some sample items within it, such as marketing, sales, HR, etc. It makes it easier for the end user to know what to expect from that filter. They could give feedback if they had different expectations and it can be easily tailored to their needs at this stage. This is also the opportunity to tackle any issues around number of filters and any important filters that were missed.

However, it does not mean that every request should be acquiesced to. On the contrary, if they were not identified in the prior steps, the question here is why a new filter should be added at this stage. A way to manage that is to take note of the additional filter and consider it for inclusion in a subsequent iteration, if it makes sense and aligns with the principles already discussed. As long as the end user feels like they are being involved, not everything they say needs to be included by default. The power of the wireframe is not just in setting expectations, it is part of the change management journey. The journey to engagement and partnership.

The charts in the wireframes are a little more detailed and there can be a wide range of interpretation needed when distilling the outputs from the "What does the end user need to see?" in the scenario mapping exercise. Multiple charts may be needed to fulfill the needs of the end user as they pertain to each of these questions. Not only that, but the level of detail in the answer can vary to a large degree from "I need to see a pie chart" to "I need to see a breakdown of all the products by category and, beside that, I want to see how they have been performing over the past year by month." Neither of these is wrong, but there is quite a gap in detail. These gaps can be bridged by a knowledge of data visualization but, should that expertise not exist, it is reasonable to work with the end user in talking through some of the charting options, especially when using supporting visuals, like showing the different available chart types and seeing which one fits the need the best.

Data visualization can be a rabbit hole. Yes, there are optimal charts for any given scenario. But, as soon as picking the exact right chart starts to hinder adoption, then it has gone too far. Chart selection can cause unnecessary friction with the end users. This is the primary reason for the scenario mapping emphasis on what the user wants to see. The end users are involved in the chart selection process. Although it may mean the best chart for the job is not selected, that is an acceptable trade-off for more end user engagement. Charts can always be improved upon later. As is becoming evident, there are a number of trade-offs in service of adoption, and adoption must remain top of mind when these decisions are being made. If adoption is at risk, are there alternative solutions that could reasonably be available through iterations? Does everything have to be nailed in the exact desired way on the first iteration? Of course not!

Even if the initial chart selections are not ideal, they can be tweaked on each iteration. Maybe the first iteration has a pie chart in it, because that is what the user felt strongly about. Maybe iteration two has replaced the pie chart with a bar chart, depending on how the user feels about it.

Another option is to replicate the data on a tab but visualize it differently on another tab. This would result in the end user being able to have the tab with the charts they like and an alternate tab, that has the same information, but it is using different chart types. The user has the comfort of working with familiar charts while also being able to kick the tires on potentially more optimal charts. All the while, they lose nothing. They can become familiar with a faster path to insight and, hopefully, see the value in it. That being the case, they will be more open to exploring other chart options for them in future.

Wireframing tools

There are a great many tools available for creating wireframes. From the super low-tech whiteboard all the way to Adobe XD, with the Dashboard Wireframe Kit being somewhere in the middle. The question is, which tool best supports the organization and collaboration. A whiteboard is excellent when people can be in a room together, but less ideal for remote teams. Anyone can contribute and collaborate on a whiteboard, physical location not being a barrier of course.

A tool like Adobe XD, however, is not something everyone has access to. It is a truly excellent tool for creating compelling high-fidelity wireframes, but if there is a need for others to be able to edit and tweak it then it is not so ideal. Example wireframes are available on the book website.

PowerPoint has much appeal. Most people have it already, or a means of being able to edit PowerPoint slides. That is a big plus. There is also a range of fidelity possible in the tool. It satisfies many of the needs but also lacks some specificity to wireframing and the common visual templates that would be specific to dashboards. With the right set of templates, PowerPoint is fast, collaborative, and widely used. A set of templates can overcome some of the challenges of using it for wireframing. Added to that, there is no additional cost need to procure the tool since most organizations already have enterprise-wide licensing. Visit the book website for a free template that can be leveraged for creating wireframes in PowerPoint. This template is all that is needed to get started with wireframing right away and start collaborating with end users in designing their ideal dashboards.

For those that have a need for a tactile experience when wireframing, such as using a whiteboard or sticky notes, then the Dashboard Wireframe Kit is the ideal solution. It blends the benefits of the more free-form approach of a whiteboard but is tailored to dashboards, aligns specifically to the process in this book, and has the added benefit that it gives participants a sense of confidence that a best practice tool is being leveraged.

Do not wait, start now

All the concepts and principles in this chapter are useless unless applied. The beauty of wireframing is that it can be a carrier for introducing many of the concepts, not just from this chapter, but from the entire book. Wireframes can be the primary delivery vehicle for interaction with the end users in a relatable and engaging way.

Indeed, if there is a challenge in running interviews and the requirements process, then wireframing can be an effective proxy for working with end users. It is not a replacement for effective requirements gathering but can help ease into deploying the whole process for the first few iterations.

It is much easier to start that journey of change by just adding in wireframing to an existing process and gradually expanding from there than it is to completely replace an existing process with a new one. When applied correctly, a wireframe can include the questions the end user needs to answer, the actions they will take and, naturally, how it will look. There are gaps here, however, such as the data assessment and other aspects of the process but it is a start to the journey and not the destination.

Crafting the vision for insight is a vitally important step to get right. Risk can be reduced, expectation managed, and alignment on outcomes can be agreed upon. From UI principles to being a bridge from requirements gathering, it is a truly powerful way to bring people along the journey of change. Start applying these principles now and see the rapid impact this will have in end user engagement and, ultimately, adoption.

09

Managing change

STORY

Fewer things have had a bigger impact on analytics adoption than having an appreciation for change management and how resistant people can be to change. I have often gone into a project for a client with the assumption that they are all on board with the goal of leveraging data to improve their business. Indeed, my expectation is that there would be excitement at the prospect of what data can do for them! Well, more often that not, that is an incorrect perspective.

On one such occasion, the client, who was a marketing leader within their organization, was fully on board with the vision and was the lead sponsor for measuring and ROI from their marketing spend. He wanted to answer the question of what impact and return the organization was getting from their marketing dollars. To truly understand that, more than marketing data was needed. He owned the marketing data, so there was no issue in getting access to that. However, to measure the impact of marketing campaigns as they pertained to sales, he needed access to sales data, which was owned by the sales department.

Well, it turns out that sales did not want to share their data. As I was to learn, it was a bit of a political situation. Sales were attributing all their success to their own work and efforts. It was not in their interest to acknowledge the marketing department as it would split their commissions. After several attempts there was seemingly no way to overcome the problem and the project languished for a time until it was escalated to the executive leadership, who mandated the sharing of data across departments. It was a lesson in understanding the landscape first. Before assuming everyone is excited to leverage data, be aware that there are probably big boulders to address first.

Every organization has politics, siloes, and vested interests. Whether people like to admit it or not, they are there. Rather than just bumping up against them and being reactive in dealing with them, taking a proactive approach is a far more successful means of overcoming them or, at least, navigating them. These issues can be especially worthy of consideration when working with data. Data presents a reality that may differ from existing perspectives and not necessarily because the data is the truth but how the data is interpreted and the formulas behind the metrics also. For these reasons, an approach to change is needed as part of ensuring successful adoption.

Consider a small data team that consists of a BI manager, a dashboard developer, and a data engineer. Their mandate is to provide "actionable insights" to their department. Assuming they deliver on that mandate, how is the organization going to adapt to the change of having this new stream of insights coming into it? Who is performing the "gap analysis" to identify what the barriers are to adopting these insights, and what steps will be needed to overcome them? Who is going to help advocate for the change and support the execution of the vision? How is the organization going to instill the outcomes into their culture for lasting impact and change?

When laid out like this, it seems logical and almost common sense. To illustrate the point, there could be a few scenarios that unfold. For this mental exercise there are two to explore. Scenario one is the data team ends up producing a dashboard with insights that are not transformative. Indeed, no one is interested, it looks cluttered, it is not designed for any specific persona, and there will be little to no positive impact by releasing the dashboard within their department. On the contrary, there may be negative impact in releasing something of low value with people wondering why the team exists if this is an example of what they can expect from the team. The perception can be that data professionals are well paid and, whether fair or not, the bar may be set higher for what such individuals should be producing.

With this first scenario there is little need for managing change, as the impact is going to be low. It is almost as though the belief is not there that data can transform an organization, that transformational change is not possible. Or, at least, the vision is lacking the possibility that change is even possible. This can absolutely be an unconscious belief held by the team. Whether unconscious or otherwise, the team is not equipped to make an impact.

In another possible scenario, scenario two, the team knocks it out of the park and produces insights that are epic in nature and can transform not only how their department does business but also their whole company. They surfaced data that indicates a potential market opportunity and customer segment that will double the company revenue if acted upon immediately. There is a customer segment that the organization has been underserving but that has consistently made large product purchases. The segment has been undermarketed to, while that same segment produces the highest sales margins. The data also indicates it costs the least amount of marketing dollars to convert this customer segment to buyers.

Scenario two is the ideal state for the team. It is also why the team was hired by the organization—to produce insights that will ultimately generate more revenue for the company. The team has done everything right in terms of their roles and responsibilities. However, when they try to share the insight, they meet considerable resistance. The VP of marketing disregards their findings, saying that the identified customer segment is not a real one and the data is probably not accurate. The VP does not like being told how to do marketing, basically, and did not like having the marketing systems shut down for several days. There is really no rationale that will get the VP on board at this stage. Since the VP was not part of the journey, was not given opportunity to give input, they have become a detractor rather than a champion. They may actively cast aspersions on the data team. The implication, from the VP's perspective, is that the VP missed this market opportunity and may have cost the company millions in lost opportunity costs over the years. It is not a good look for the VP and self-interest and self-preservation will likely take priority.

In addition, the VP for sales likes the lack of transparency about what customers are most profitable as it allows for obfuscation of commissions and attribution of sales opportunities. The result is there are two senior stakeholders that do not want these insights to see the light of day and may actively work against them.

Of course, none of this should be the concern of the data team but, nonetheless, it is clearly a barrier. All their work will not be able to impact the strategy of the business. So, the question becomes, who should own solving this problem? How can these issues be overcome? What could they have done differently to have made it work out?

The answer to this problem is not unique and existed long before the field of BI and analytics emerged. Change management methodologies have been tackling these challenges for many years. Indeed, even before change management methodologies were formalized, these issues were being tackled by highly effective communicators who understood the barrier that bringing people on a journey can entail.

Fortunately, there are many approaches to change available now. Change management is a process. There are excellent change management methodologies that offer various approaches to introducing change within organizations and ensuring adoption of whatever is being introduced or is happening. Ideally, a change process would generate excitement for the change and clearly outline the benefits of the change. The impacts of the change may necessitate shifts in current business processes, roles, responsibilities, and organizational structures.

Approaches to change

Change in the enterprise is a well-understood field. Some change methodologies place a primary focus on people, as they are the drivers or resistors to change ultimately. Others place emphasis on technology, processes, and systems. Some of the most popular models include Kotter's 8-step process for leading change, the ADKAR model, and the Kübler-Ross model. They each take a different approach to change.

It is worth being familiar with these models as they each have something to offer in support of increasing adoption, regardless of the type of change, be it dashboards or changing organizational structure. They are comprehensive in their approach and take commitment and dedication to execute.

Following a process is one thing, but it is also important to understand why it works. To gain that understanding, a quick breakdown of a relevant change methodology will be helpful. One of the most popular change frameworks, the 8-step strategy from John Kotter (1996), includes the following:

1 Create a sense of urgency: enable others to share in the vision and why rapid action is needed

2 Build a guiding coalition: gather a group of people or "change champions" that can help evangelize the change

3 Form a strategic vision and initiatives: connect the current state to the desired future state with an action plan and necessary steps identified to get there

4 Enlist a volunteer army: to enable a significant transformation, a suitably large number of people is needed to buy into the vision but also to march it in the same direction

5 Enable action by removing barriers: identify and remove any blockers to success such as processes, inefficient workflows, and any unnecessary hindrances

6 Generate short-term wins: share and communicate small successes to keep energy up and to show progress

7 Sustain acceleration: continue pushing, following success after success—the momentum of credibility and improvement becomes a driving force

8 Institute change: incorporate the change into the organizational culture so that old habits are replaced

There is a reason why people dedicate their careers to the topic of change management—it can be entirely capable of consuming an entire workday with no time left for anything else. Not that that is a bad thing, as it is a high-value occupation. The challenge is for the individual, or smaller teams, to be able to have an approach to change without having the expertise to effect that change. It is a challenge that plagues data professionals and departments, whether they are aware of it or not. The simple reality is that while data professionals are equipped to work with data, they are not always equipped to make lasting organizational impact with that data.

STORY

There was a time when I had no clue about change management and thought that everyone would be excited to learn about data and insights as they pertained to their business. On one occasion, I was running a workshop for a large enterprise client. There were about 15 participants and two senior executives participating. The reason given for why the workshop was needed was to align the team on what to expect from using data in their team.

Honestly, it did not even dawn on me to ask why alignment was needed. Also, why was an external consultant being asked to do that and not someone internal? I treated it like every other type of session where I would take more of a training and teaching approach on the process of how to create insights. About 20 minutes into the session, talking about data visualization best practices, one of the executives mentioned that he knew all this stuff and kind of scoffed. I must say, it unsettled me a bit, as I had not had such a response before.

With a hit to my confidence, I carried on, trying my best to keep it interesting and engaging. I had quickly moved on to talking about the impact data can have in organizations. However, only ten minutes later, the same executive stood up and said to me, in front of all the attendees "Whatever your name is, this is all rubbish and a waste of my time." He proceeded to walk out of the room, clearly enraged. I was shattered. This was surely the end of my career, certainly the end of the relationship with this large client.

While I was contemplating how to proceed, the other executive stayed in her seat, looked me in the eye and said "Thank God he is gone, now we can have some fun!" The first thing that struck me was, what hornets' nest had I walked into? While glad that the situation was defused in the moment, I resolved to not let something like that happen again. I could not walk into situations where I knew nothing of the internal politics and points of friction that might exist.

Change management lite

What is needed is a "lite" version of change management. An approach that data professionals can follow without the need to have deep expertise in any of the excellent models that are out there. Naturally, there needs to be a compromise between completeness and accessibility. If it is too comprehensive then data professionals may not be able or willing to implement it. Conversely, if it is too "lite" then it may not be effective. Again, simplicity needs to rule the day when adapting best practice, yet unfamiliar, frameworks.

To make life simple, consider these three phases of change:

1 Pre-change

2 Change

3 Post-change

Pre-change

Prior to implementing any change, it is necessary first to identify what the status quo is before making any plans to change it. A rapid assessment of where things currently are will help build a foundation of understanding prior to making a plan for what the vision can look like. It is natural for people to resist change. But it is not just people that change may need to be applied to.

All barriers to the change should be identified and a simple framework to use is to identify the barriers, blockers, and gaps to efficiency across people, process, technology, and data. Everything must be on the table for consideration about what is holding the organization back. Only then can a true transformation and change take place. If it is well known a certain person's behaviors will block a project, why execute the project at all if the behavior is not changed or there is some other means to overcome it? There may be a legacy process in place that adds hours of manual effort which could be replaced by a more efficient process. Whatever the gaps might be, they must be identified.

Not only is it important to identify the gaps but communicating those gaps to the intended audience is vital to prepare them for the change to come. They need to get behind "the why"—why there is the need for change and how maintaining the status quo is not tenable. Communicating the pain helps to set up what the benefits can be of making a change. This can take time but making the effort to communicate early will help get people on board later when the change takes place. They will know to expect it and what is in it for them.

With the intended audience being brought up to speed on the problems at hand and the benefits of addressing them, there is one more key ingredient that should go into the communications plan. A sense of urgency. Indeed, if everyone is aware of what the inefficiencies are costing the organization, why would anyone want to delay making changes for the best? Especially if those changes can positively impact the individual. It seems almost an untenable position to take to not want to make the necessary changes. Clearly articulating the benefits to the people on what they stand to gain from the change will help reduce and lower the barriers and resistance. The faster it happens, the better their lives will be! Having fixed timelines for the change will help increase the sense of needing to act now and not put it off any longer. The more communication around this, the better.

Change

The second phase is to actually apply the change that was communicated in the prior phase. Rather than talking about the change, this is when it happens and begins to roll out. Care must be taken as it is rather easy to talk about change, but when people start to be impacted by the change they may start to react to it and still resist it. Change brings fear, confusion, and uncertainty. Even when everyone knows it was coming, there is still risk involved. It requires new behaviors to be learned, understanding the new way of doing things, and adjusting to new processes. Certainly, greater preparation helps alleviate some of the challenges but, oftentimes, there may not be the luxury of time to give people lots of lead-up for the change.

This phase marks the moving of the team or organization from the old state to the new. Ample time must be made available to people who are in this transitioning state to give them necessary support, training, and communication. This guidance will help them navigate to the envisioned state. Throughout the process, there are continuous reminders of the rationale for the change and how the benefits of the change will be making life easier for them. The intent is that, even though the transition is uncomfortable, it will be worth getting through it to realize the benefits at the end.

Preparation and planning are key to this phase. Having the necessary training materials, support documentation, and executive support makes the difference between success and failure. As issues arise, and likely they will, there are predefined paths to address them or escalate them to the appropriate person, as necessary.

Post-change

The final stage, the post-change, does not leave people to their own devices after the change has been implemented. The change must be instilled in the culture. It cannot have been just a flash in the pan, sort of a one-time deal that worked great for a single point in time but did not stick around for the long term. It should be like the punch of a boxer that aims to punch beyond the intended target. The change must become established as the new way and the new normal.

Ideally, making the change sticky, in a rapid and agile way, is important but should not take months. In the modern era, especially with data driving business strategy, change should be the standard, not a thing that happens every now and again that annoyingly upturns the status quo. Rather, change is the new standard, and the days of long-lasting behaviors, workflows, and inflexible processes are in the rearview mirror. Businesses continually reinvent themselves at speed and with agility. The ear of the business should be to the ground and actively listening for change through their data, eager and willing to rapidly implement and adjust to any change that is necessary.

Application of the steps

To understand how the steps could be applied in a BI context, consider the data team from the start of the chapter. They are hitting the reset button and will leverage the three stages from the pre-change and change to the final stage, the post-change. The team want to introduce new marketing insights into the company. The marketing organization has relied on many disparate systems for their activities, from managing their advertising campaigns to tracking customer conversions. They have struggled with having a single view of their customer and the entire customer journey. Having this view of the customer will have a large impact on the business as a whole.

First, in the pre-change step, the team need to establish and baseline the current way of doing things so that they can change it. It is not only the marketing department that will see an impact but the entire organization, from the sales teams to the finance and accounting teams. Since the impact is going to be so broad, there must be executive and management support and active engagement. Potential gaps need to be identified as well as understanding what individuals will need greater levels of support throughout the change. From a series of conversations, several specific individuals are identified as being the most impacted by the change, and they must be communicated with early and often. In this case, they include the VPs of marketing and of sales.

The benefit of changing this status quo must be communicated to anyone who is going to be impacted by the change. The data team must demonstrate how the benefits will outweigh the disruption of the change. They come up with a communications plan and execute it over the course of several weeks. The result is that all the impacted teams are aware of the need for the change, when the change is coming, and what the benefits of the change are going to be. The value proposition is abundantly clear. There will be disruption. The VP of marketing understands there will be an outage of the current marketing tools for up to three days but also has a clear and documented appreciation for what that will look like and the benefits to be realized after the disruption. The executive team needs to be involved with the VP of sales to change how they incentivize the sales team so the transformation is not seen as a threat but rather an opportunity to spend more time on activities that will make more commissions for the entire sales team.

While many departments will be impacted, stage two, the change stage, requires the biggest shift from the marketing team as they will be transitioning marketing platforms from many to a select few. While it will take a while to transition to the new tools, the benefits of the change are that it will save the marketing team a bunch of hours every week. That is not to mention all the great customer insights they will be getting from the change that will increase revenues for the whole business. With the technology shift underway, it is a time of confusion, but the data team can support with training and help bring the marketing team along the journey, all the while emphasizing the benefits they will realize. Dashboard wireframes are used to paint the picture of the insights they will be receiving once the new systems are in place and enough data has been gathered to be valuable, which could take several months. The sales team are undergoing the shift to a different operating model and incentivization structure, and are supported accordingly.

Eventually, the new systems and processes are in place and the new way of business has been operating. The change now needs to stick, there cannot be a reversion back to the old ways. What is especially important is that individuals do not revert to the old tools they used because they are more comfortable with them. This would somewhat negate the benefit of the transition, but it is a natural thing for people to do, favoring the comfortable user experience, even if it is not to their immediate benefit, i.e., comfort over value. It is a risk that must be managed, and the necessary support structures need to be in place, like weekly informal meetings, regular training opportunities, and easily accessible documentation.

With the new approach adopted for a time, the results are measured, and the realized benefits are evangelized throughout the organization and continually highlighted by the management. While it can take time for the benefits to filter through and have an impact, smaller wins are noted and shared throughout the weeks that pass.

Praise is heaped on the marketing team and they are kept front and center on weekly calls where the new marketing leads that come in are attributed to the new approach.

Key takeaways

There are a number of important elements to note from the above example. First and foremost, it was the executive sponsorship that was necessary in order to get the VPs of sales and marketing on board, and any necessary compensations and organizations models adjusted, which could only happen with executive support. If the data team had skipped that part they would have ended up in trouble again and be dealing with the political impact of not taking a more holistic approach to the change. It is better to assume that, for a change effort to succeed, some execute support is necessary. This is especially true of any strategic endeavors that are likely to have greater impact and, potentially, might ruffle a few feathers.

For many organizations, the operating models that currently exist have been around for many years and have not evolved. So, there may be significant gaps for the organization to be able to execute the actions suggested by their newly emerging insights. This makes change management even more necessary and vital. It is akin to swapping out the engine of an old car with one that is modern with lots and lots of power. Yet the rest of the car cannot support the increased output of the new engine. The axles are unable to deal with the torque, the wheels are not strong enough to cope with the additional speed, and the exhaust system is not designed to handle the increased flow. While it is a great start to swap the engine for a better one, it is just one piece of the machine that needs to be replaced and modernized. Otherwise, it is the weakest link that will determine the performance of the car. It will not make much progress if the wheels come off! It will be a powerful car without the means of delivering that power to the road.

This car analogy is highly relevant to the influx of data professionals graduating with degrees and expertise in advanced analytics, BI, and data engineering. Without the proper support and knowledge, they will build a powerful engine but the power of it will never truly move the business along without the other pieces in place.

Tying back to the process

The start of this book introduced the strategy template, and a subsequent chapter introduced the agile process that should be leveraged. While it is not intended to be comprehensive, the strategy template has an area for change management. It makes accommodations for indicating gaps that must be addressed across people, process, technology, and data. Each area identified will need a change plan and discussion around how to achieve the change. In part, another reason is to create awareness that change is important for data projects and a data professional can point to this template as a best practice for what is required for success. Failing that, hire a consultant and point to them as the scapegoat for needing a change plan!

The process outlined in the book is, to a degree, a means of executing change, as it pertains to adopting insights via a dashboard. It is certainly specific to the field of data and is not broad enough to be used for any change plan for any type of project. Additionally, it is not a comprehensive approach to change and should not be viewed as such. What it will do is equip data professionals with enough knowledge and change awareness to make them more effective in achieving the changes needed to have a greater chance that their dashboards and insights can be adopted without the need for years of study. The stages of the process roughly map to the phases of change.

The pre-change aligns with the requirements stage of the process, which includes completing the strategy template. Since the main effort is to gather requirements, and conducting interviews in support of that, there is opportunity to identify the change gaps that exist but to also inform the participants what change is coming and what the benefits are. This can be achieved when communicating with the stakeholders and end users via email during the inception of the project. An example might look like:

Dear marketing team,

Over the past year many of you have made recommendations as to what you want to see happen with our customer data and ways to improve our customer insights. Your feedback has been heard and it is time to transform our marketing insights!

First and foremost, the most consistent challenge has been that it takes a lot of manual effort to measure campaign performance. For some of you it takes several hours out of your week, up to five hours in some cases. Even after doing that, the quality of the data that is there is not always trustworthy and only certain insights can be gleaned.

Second, all of you stated that requesting access to the data is slow and takes several attempts. When you run a survey, it can sometimes take weeks to get the results back and, after such a time, it might be too late to take action on.

Well, you have been heard! The first steps are being taken to tackle these challenges. It is going to be a bumpy road for a while as new systems are put in place, but it will result in getting direct access to customer insights. Gone will be the days of manual effort—your insights will be automated and updated on a daily basis. Since the marketing team will own the new tools, the need to make data requests is gone. No more waiting, no more dependencies, just great insights!

To get there, we will be setting up a new platform in the coming weeks and it will mean we will have no data for about two weeks. Nothing at all—a complete black out. Following that, it will take a few weeks for the new data to start coming in before your shiny new dashboards will be fully functioning and saving you hours of repetitive manual work every week.

Thank you for your patience and commitment to improving our data—it will be worth the wait!

Regards,

Director of marketing insights

There can be more emails like this prior to the change happening, as well as events like a "lunch and learn" and workshops that are available should people want to attend. The net effect is that people know that the change is coming, what the impacts will be and, ultimately, the benefits. The design stage is a continuation of the pre-launch, but starts to make it more real by sharing the wireframes and the vision for what the interface is going to look like. People can connect more with what the benefits of the change will be when they see what the interface will look like.

The development stage is where the transition to the change phase happens for some of the audience, the ones involved in user acceptance testing. The majority of end users will feel the change during the launch step in the adoption stage. It is the reason why the launch step is quite a detailed set of activities, as care must be taken to ensure adequate support is available.

Finally, the post-change is affected by both the measurement step as well as with the next iteration of the dashboard. Measurement tracks whether the change is taking place at the desired pace, and if it is not, why not? Are there any special considerations that are needed for the next iteration and, if so, should emphasis be placed elsewhere? It is necessary to take a pause before jumping into executing the overall strategy without making adjustments and tweaks based on how the participants are responding to change. It is possible that there is more capacity for change, and it can be accelerated in the next iteration. Of course, people might be struggling, and the pace needs to slow down to accommodate that. Whatever the case, taking a pulse on how people are feeling will allow for any necessary adjustments and tailoring of the process.

Ongoing change

Change is rarely easy and, more often than not, a plan of action will be needed. It is better to assume a change plan is needed for any BI and analytics undertaking. While the desire is to focus on the work at hand, in this case creating insights that will be surfaced through a dashboard, it is preferable to temper that focus and divert some attention to the change steps outlined in this chapter. Since there are only so many hours in a day, some time sacrifice has to be made in order to accommodate the additional activities for change management. Those trade-offs might include a reduction in the BVQs addressed in the current iteration or, perhaps, fewer personas are catered to.

Whatever the accommodations are, managing change is a vital addition and consideration for any data project. It is almost folly to not have some degree of change awareness in the majority of situations. Adoption does not happen by accident. It requires a plan, communication, and feedback. Over time it becomes easier, but it can be especially difficult in stagnant organizations. The more stagnant, the more the need to use communication in order to manage the friction. In such situations, there is an argument to be made for the first iteration of a dashboard to only be focused on change and communications, with no actual outputs other than a clear understanding of what is to come in the next iteration.

With that in mind, the next chapter tackles who should own adoption, the roles and responsibilities to drive adoption, and what role the various flavors of self-service can play in supporting the adoption of insight.

Reference

Kotter, J. 1996. *Leading Change: An action plan from the world's foremost expert on business leadership*. Boston, MA: Harvard Business Review Press

10

Adoption and ownership

STORY

Some organizations are just better set up to deliver insights. Some are structured so the ball can continue to be kicked down the road. The latter was the type of organization I found myself supporting a few years into my analytics career. The organization was a behemoth. You name a department and they had it. An IT department for each department? You got it! Why not!? There were firewalls left, right, and center. Data siloes existed not just by department, but were beautifully matrixed by geography, product category, and by customer type.

Looking back, I am glad I got out of that project alive. It was next to impossible to get anything accomplished and, having spoken extensively to a number of the employees there, that was a shared view. The primary reason appeared to be ownership and responsibility. Given the degree of organizational matrices, it was easy to pass the buck from one group to another for who was responsible for what. For example, when trying to track down a definitive unique identifier for the customer field, there was no standard. Each IT department had a different way of tracking it so there was no way to connect the customer data across departments. Everyone was quick to point out that so-and-so department did not use such-and-such an approach. Ultimately, no one really cared enough, and the mountain of inertia was just too great for a small team to overcome.

I learned two things from that project. First, organizational structures matter for delivering insight and they may become insurmountable. Second, assigning ownership and responsibility to adoption is vital for success.

Adoption has become the holy grail of analytics and BI. Some years ago, the term was rarely used, but it is extremely common now and most data conferences touch on the topic. It has many flavors and there are some popular spinoffs from it, such as data literacy and data culture. Ultimately, the goal is adoption—to have as many people as possible in an organization interpreting and acting appropriately on data. To have data driving the organization's strategy and the employees all working off a tiered and cascaded set of insights that both inform the strategy but also execute against it.

Indeed, adoption has become such a focus that many tools try to address it in their own ways. Several BI platforms emphasize self-service as a partial panacea to address barriers to adoption. Analytics hubs take the route of improving discovery and access to insights as a primary factor in increasing adoption. Data literacy programs take a people and enablement focus to addressing the challenge.

Adoption is a primary focus because it is the last mile of the journey and it has been a difficult journey. So much goes into delivering insight and so much can go wrong along the way that, maybe understandably, adoption was not top of mind until it needed to be or, at least, it became such an obvious gap that it became visible because of all the great work that went before it.

The sad reality is that a well-structured data warehouse can sit and metaphorically gather dust if adoption is low. The best data science models can output compelling insights but end up wasting CPU cycles if no one is acting on those insights. Imagine all the wasted infrastructure out there that is churning though data that is not fully being taken advantage of. The tracks are laid but no passengers are being carried along them.

Specialization in data and analytics has led to narrowly focused roles and expertise, and the necessary perspective can be lost, forgetting the "So what?" Sure, a highly performant data model is great, but so what, if the end user keeps using a spreadsheet and never touches that model? It is easy to get caught up in the details of data, but the wider perspective must be maintained. Adoption must be kept top of mind for any stage of the data journey. There must be a continuous focus on the "So what?" across all stages of the data pipeline and spanning the attention of all the individuals involved, no matter the activity or role they play.

Indeed, the measure of success for any BI, IT, or analytics department should be the degree to which their work is adopted by end users. But that is not enough, there must also be impact. Much like how marketing departments seek to attribute certain marketing efforts to increases in revenue, data teams should seek to establish how the insights they deliver impact the business. Such an approach firmly places an emphasis on if and how people are using their data, what they might need to do differently, and whether there is a sufficient return on investment in data.

All too often, money is dumped into data projects without a thought on how the return on investment is going to be tracked. Even having a data strategy in place at the top levels of an organization does not guarantee adoption. It ultimately comes down to accountability and responsibility for adoption, at all levels of decision-making and roles involving data. No longer can resources be blindly dropped into the data budget black hole. Every dollar should be assigned a corresponding return dollar, or multiple thereof. Adoption does not happen by accident; it is a deliberate and conscious process that holds people accountable while also providing corresponding incentivization. Only then can the promise of data be fully realized and the vision of "actionable insights" have a true impact on the organization.

STORY

One of the most transformational analytics projects I was involved on was also one of my first projects. I had the good fortune of seeing an individual at work who deeply understood how to drive adoption. Let's call him Atrick. Like many organizations, the client had data and had produced several reports over the years that were made available to the end users. However, they were rarely used.

To better understand what was happening, Atrick and I had a series of one-on-one interviews with over twenty employees in a specific department that had a higher proportion of reports made for them over the years. We heard many of the typical challenges people experience with reporting, such as the questions they care about not being answered and it taking too long for the data to refresh. All pertinent issues, for sure. But in one interview the interviewee mentioned, almost as an aside, that it did not help them hit their Christmas bonus target so they could maximize their bonus payout.

To me, at the time, it seemed like an innocuous comment. However, Atrick thought differently. At every subsequent interview, it became one of Atrick's leading questions: "Tell me about your Christmas bonus over the past years—did you hit your target?" The common answer was that people generally picked up about 20 percent of that bonus and left a chunk of it on the table. Of course, when asked, they obviously wanted to maximize that number. That extra 80 percent might have been the difference between whether they had a family holiday or some other large spend, or not.

I figured Atrick was on to something and we should design the reports so that they supported reaching their targets more effectively. However, Atrick was not of that mind. Atrick spoke to the project sponsor, a senior executive, and said the problem was not poor reporting, it was a misalignment between employee goals and corporate goals. The reports represented employee goals—they helped them do their jobs. Their Christmas bonuses aligned with corporate goals, which the employees rarely attained because they were acting off information in their reports that did not align with the organizational goals.

The client ended up changing their compensation and incentive structure so that the employees, by acting on data, would be more likely to attain more, if not all, of their Christmas bonus. A year later, and a bonus cycle later, and the interviews were very different. People had more money in their pockets, could see a direct relationship between their role and corporate strategy, and knew how they could maximize their bonus for next year.

Compensation based on adoption

Organizations have many different, and well-established, ways of compensating and incentivizing employees. However, many of these can be legacy holdovers that do not excite or energize the modern enterprise that leverages data. If the vision of data is to transform an organization, then a corresponding compensation model should be in place to support and encourage leveraging and acting on data.

There are many levers that can be pulled to promote adoption of data. These levers need to be role and level appropriate and span the range of strategic, operational, and tactical. Strategic level compensation would be focused on an executive level, with a departmental or similar focus. Adoption of data would be directly measured against the impact it is having on corporate goals but also, specifically, how many people in that organization or department are leveraging data.

The operational level would take a slightly more detailed and nuanced approach to measuring adoption, as well as being more role-specific. For example, a manager level might be incentivized on how closely they are tracking to their defined KPIs. In addition, how many people in their span of control are actively accessing dashboards and taking the appropriate actions?

Going a layer deeper, to the tactical level, these individuals would be almost entirely incentivized on what actions they are taking to remediate issues highlighted by their data and tracking towards their defined metrics. It can be useful to also measure who is accessing reports and dashboards, and how often, but it should not be a shared metric that it is being tracked as people may just open it simply to tick that box but not take any resulting action.

Those may seem like obvious changes to make to an organization, but they can take a mammoth effort to implement as the impacts are far and wide-ranging. Such a change requires the involvement of human resources, finance, accounting, executive buy-in, and more. However, it is a key ingredient to the adoption recipe and cannot be ignored because it might be hard. By itself, data-aligned compensation can dramatically shift the data culture of an organization and rapidly bring awareness of the value of data to broad swathes of an organization.

Imagine a new marketing hire in an organization that tells them, on day one of their new role, that they can get an additional $500 for every measurable action taken that increases customer engagement by 0.1 percent. If the dashboard indicated the potential additional income that is feasible, it would be a highly motivating goal. This individual would be all about data! They would have a clear path and understanding on how data can increase their compensation.

Naturally, the business is not giving money away for free. Increasing customer engagement means serious returns. Everybody wins and the path to value from the executive level is maintained through to the tactical level. Once the first check hits the bank account of the new hire then things get much more real. There is a rapid financial feedback loop established for the employee where they can see the benefit of working with data in the very short term. This individual will actively help elevate the data culture and be an advocate for making decisions accordingly, from showing up to meetings with a dashboard to finding new ways of taking action and being a proactive participant in the insight design process.

Measuring adoption

For any of the above strategies to work, adoption must be measured. Or, at least, there needs to be a proxy measurement for adoption that can be tracked. This is slightly different from measuring the outcomes that are documented in the strategy template. Measuring outcomes is essential and must be part of any end of iteration approach. However, a key part of achieving the outcomes is how many people are actually working towards those outcomes, and that is where measuring adoption plays a role.

There are several ways to approach measurement. For starters, tracking the number of times an end user opens a dashboard is a simple measure. However, by itself, it may not be sufficient. Measurement of active usage would track how long a dashboard session is while it is being actively used versus the dashboard just open on a desktop for days at a time but the user not using it.

A balance between business outcomes and active usage is a great place to start measuring adoption more purely. People need to be logging into the dashboard regularly, so they are aligned to the content of the dashboard and understand that activity is important. But, more importantly, are the actions they are taking also making progress towards the dashboard strategy? This is obviously covered by the KPIs in the dashboard itself. A weighting is given to progress against the KPIs. If a user is not logging into a dashboard terribly often but their KPIs are progressing, then no one should be too upset about that. But, if the KPIs are not making progress and they are not regularly logging into the dashboard, then there might be some conversations to be had.

Ultimately, when the process is correctly applied, adoption is directly correlated to achieving the stated outcomes. The more people adopting and acting on data, the more likely the goals will be achieved, assuming they were appropriately set and actioned upon. Frequent measurement affords an opportunity to tweak and adjust. If adoption is high and the desired outcomes are not there, then maybe tweaks to the requirements are needed or perhaps the personas are off, or any number of other elements could need adjustment. Taking time to measure supplies the data needed to become more successful and provides the fodder for the strategy for the next iteration.

Technology approaches to adoption

On the topic of measurement of usage, there are several out-of-the-box ways to do this without having to do any custom development. The popular BI platforms, by and large, already provide usage tracking. Assuming the correct levels of access are in place, an admin can see who is using what dashboard, how often, and for how long. This works perfectly well in situations where there is only a single BI platform. But what about organizations that have many BI platforms? A clean way to track usage across multiple platforms is to use an analytics hub.

An analytics hub provides a single interface to access all the reports and dashboards within an organization, irrespective of what technology they are created in. What that means for the end user is that they can easily find the current reports and dashboards they use. Not only that, they can also discover reports that they might not have known existed but have data they might be interested in. Those are nice-to-have benefits but the real value comes in having an entire meta layer placed on all reports and dashboards. That layer enables measurement of adoption across all the reporting technologies that are in the hub. This feature in hubs is greatly undervalued.

Many hubs also allow reports and dashboards to be rated and reviewed so a user can see what their colleagues think about a specific dashboard. The experience is a little like buying a product from an online store, where one typically looks for the number of reviews a product has as well as the rating. It promotes trust, as users can quickly identify which assets are trusted and are regularly used and will steer clear of the ones that are less so.

Regardless of the technology used, whether custom or off the shelf, there is immense value in maintaining a meta layer of additional information and context about the overall landscape of reports and dashboards. It is almost a given for any IT, BI, or analytics department. Consider it akin to a SharePoint site or internal company portal. It is a storefront for insight.

An easy comparison to make is with Netflix. When searching for a movie, the user is not thinking about what make of cameras were used to film it or which production studio produced the movie. People might search by "comedy" or "action". They might find a movie they like and want to see what movies are similar to that. Seeing the IMDB movie rating on the interface helps them to decide whether that is a movie they would like to invest their time in watching, i.e., did other people like it? It is really not too different from how an analytics hub would perform. The user is not concerned about what technology was used to create the insights. They might search by topics like "supply chain" or "sales performance". If there is a dashboard they regularly use, perhaps they would like to see recommendations for similar dashboards. Having a view of the ratings of those dashboards will help them decide whether they want to spend their time exploring the insights in there and if their colleagues are getting value from it. Indeed, understanding who is accessing it could be a very compelling reason to explore the insights therein.

Ultimately, such technology will support the adoption of insights in a very practical and effective way by making a seamless user experience for the end user in cases where there are several BI tools in use.

A note on self-service

Self-service has become a popular term in recent years and is sometimes offered up as a panacea to adoption, whether directly or indirectly implied. Self-service in BI is giving business users direct access to tools to enable them to perform analysis on data by themselves. It is a compelling solution and can be truly powerful for the set of business users that are comfortable with the solution and are sufficiently data literate. So long as it is understood what self-service can and cannot do, that it can be a part of a wider approach to adoption, then it can have a compelling part to play in the adoption story.

Part of the reason why self-service has resonated with the business user is due to frustration in working with their IT counterparts and not getting access to the data they want and when they want it. Appropriately or not, self-service seeks to address that chasm of alignment.

However, self-service is not a one-size-fits-all solution to adoption. Incorrectly applied, as it often is, it can result in a proliferation of ungoverned reports and dashboards, a lack of standards around user experience, and inconsistent metrics, calculations, and KPI definitions. Considerable care and planning must be taken to ensure that dashboards created in this way adhere to the principles and steps outlined in this book. The temptation with self-service is the same as the temptation that faces the BI developer: to start development right away, just dive into the data and start building. That is wonderful for data exploration, but not ideal for operational reporting.

Excluding the use case of data exploration, which is a fine application for self-service, a middle ground is to leverage the process from Chapter 6 but shift the responsibilities for the steps. In the most extreme scenario, it is the business user that is following the steps in the process by themselves. This ensures there is an adherence to standards and a strategic alignment so that others may benefit from the dashboard they produce. Rather than it being a personal resource that is only used by one person, it has the opportunity to add value to a wider swathe of people.

The use cases for self-service should be carefully considered before being widely applied. As long as there is a clear understanding of what it can and cannot do, the advantages and the risks, then it can be a powerful tool. However, all too often it is applied as a panacea for low adoption and, in its current form, it is not that.

Assigning ownership and accountability

Self-service is the extreme end of ownership of the process where most, if not all, of the steps of the process from Chapter 6 are owned by the end user. It is a rare application of the process. Most of the time, the steps are either wholly owned by the BI or data team, or there is a sharing of the responsibility for the steps. The latter becomes more the case over subsequent iterations and applications of the process once people have become familiar with it. Consider a BI department that has just introduced the process and they are tasked with building a dashboard for the marketing department. It is the BI team that drives the requirements, the interviews, the data assessment, the wireframes, the development, and the launch. They are on the hook for ensuring adoption is trending in the right direction. This is especially true for early usage of the process; it is better to centralize initially while working out the kinks that are specific to the organization, before starting to delegate responsibility for aspects of the process.

Once the process has been tailored, aspects of it can be farmed out to the various parties involved in the process. In the example of the BI department, they could train the various business departments in the requirements and design stages of the process. So, the marketing department would complete the strategy template, create the end user personas, define the questions, and work with their BI team colleagues to conduct a data assessment on what would work for a first iteration. Based on that feedback, the marketing team could then wireframe how they envision their dashboard.

This is like a hybridized form of self-service. The stakeholders get more agency over what they want and, in so doing, start to gain an appreciation for the challenges of working with data. They also design what the output will look like, which results in less misalignment and fewer unmet expectations. Since they have more agency, the mentality of throwing a request at the wall is reduced and a sense of partnership takes its place. The process is more akin to a series of handoffs along a journey, a journey that has a shared vision and desired outcomes.

It is far too easy to shoot off an email to the responsible team with a cursory description of what is desired. With such little detail, it is no wonder many organizations experience low data adoption numbers. The flip side is that the dashboard requestor must now take greater responsibility and they may not be willing to do so. In such situations, it may be preferable to keep ownership of the process with one team.

Yet another benefit of sharing responsibility for the process is that the BI or IT team will have more time available to do the development work, which they can create from a clear set of documented requirements. Indeed, many BI and IT departments are so backlogged that they operate in a reactive mode. Freeing up some of their time may afford the space to be more proactive in certain activities, such as being able to focus on data quality, acquiring new sources to enrich existing data, and provide training to more departments on how to partner in creating greater and more impactful insights.

Structures for adoption

Extending the concept of the hybrid self-serve approach to the process, it could also be materialized in an organizational structure. More specifically, a team of individuals could take ownership of executing and managing the handoffs of the process and directly running some parts of the process. For example, such a group might sit between IT and the various business functions. They work with the business on the requirements stage and validate the BVQs against the available data. The team would then create the wireframes and validate them with the business and sync with the BI/IT department, so they are aware of what is coming down the pipe. It is a centralized approach to delivering insight.

Another approach would be to have separate teams for each stage of the process. It is still centralized but there would be individual teams, within this group, that specialize in each stage of the process. For example, there is a team that specializes in the requirements gathering. They would develop deep expertise in it, given their specialization. This would lead to more rapid and precise requirements and the team would be more agile than a team that would be handling the process end-to-end.

A different team would just focus on design. Like a UI/UX team in a software project, they would be adept at developing comprehensive and interactive wireframes, both low fidelity and high fidelity. The team would have access to specialized software and tools to accelerate the wireframing process and get closer to what the end result would look like. It would also serve to have more detailed requirements to pass on to the team handling the development phase.

The development team would function like a typical enterprise team does but with the addition of being able to take advantage of the outputs from both the requirements and design phases with all the details that come with them. This would also address the occasional challenge that some developers are not keen on driving user interviews. Or, they may be keen, but their interview style is not a net benefit to the effort. A rapport can be built with the design and requirements teams that are the front-of-stage people skilled at interacting with the business. The development team is the only team in this scenario that would not need to be "market" facing. They can do what they do best and focus on data and coding. With such a specialized design team, the developers will have an abundance of material to base their development on and would not need to interact with the end users.

The final team would be focused on adoption. If any stage is more focused on change management it is this one, although they all have their part to play. This team could also be the same as the requirements team, as they will need much of the same skillset, though it could be a separate team if the organizational scale is there. They take all the packaged up work the development team has completed and drive the launch of the dashboard, and are especially interested in training and enablement sessions to give the end users every opportunity to feel comfortable and make the new dashboard part of their role.

The federated, or decentralized, approach places the expertise for delivering the process in each department, as needed. The marketing department would have a team, as would sales, HR, and any department that makes, or should make, regular use of data. The primary advantage is that each team develops deep specialization in the domain that they serve and would effectively become, if they were not already, subject matter experts in that area. The challenge can be that this structure may create more data silos across departments.

The final structure is a mix between centralized and decentralized. Each department has its own team but there is a centralized core team, like a center of excellence, that maintains standards, makes all the data accessible across the teams, provides training, and many other functions that would keep alignment between the groups. The core team would make updates and adjustments to the process and handle activities that overcome the silo effect of decentralized teams. Each team handles the application of the process for their own department, so they still maintain the depth of subject matter expertise while overcoming the negative aspects of limited access to data.

Scaled-down ownership

There are several ways to assign accountability to adoption. The previous section addressed it at scale, but what about individual accountability or for smaller teams and organizations where there is simply not the scale to support dedicated teams to drive adoption? The reader of this book might find themselves taking the responsibility for adoption or it might be someone on their team that is given the task.

Naturally, there is only so much one person can do, but not all activities are equal in impact. Anyone who is in the business of crafting insights for others should first be asking themselves what the outcomes are and how they will be realized, i.e., completing the strategy template detailed at the start of the book. Such a focus forces the data professional to consider the "So what?" and how important adoption is going to be. Of course, giving the individual some incentivization is likely going to have a more profound effect on their adherence to the steps in the process to drive towards the intended outcomes.

Perhaps the employee already has some performance-related incentives. Replacing one of those with one related to adoption is an option. An example might be to measure the customer satisfaction scores (where customer is the end user) of consumers of the dashboards the employee was involved in. Another might be to track the usage of their dashboards versus the desired adoption target. Whatever the specific performance metric is, just placing an emphasis on adoption will already start to yield benefits, not to mention the impact it has on the wider data culture. When more and more people are leveraging data as part of their compensation, there will be a corresponding shift in the culture as a whole.

What gets measured, gets managed

Ultimately, as Peter Drucker is famous for saying: "What gets measured, gets managed." This rings very true for adoption. Just the act of assigning ownership and management of adoption will increase the awareness and yield more impact to the business. Assigning responsibility to adoption is the cornerstone to any analytics and BI function, regardless of the scale and structure.

Adoption is the new frontier of data. Organizations that have succeeded in evolving their data culture are the same ones that placed an emphasis on adoption, making data part of every meeting, every decision, and any strategic goal. Indeed, without an approach to ownership of adoption, why would a team undertake any analytics endeavor without first having an agreed set of roles and responsibilities that will result in the maximum adoption possible for their undertaking? One of the fastest ways to produce a mountain of low-value dashboards and reports is to dive into development without a plan around the who, how, and why.

Whether small or large scale, start with an adoption goal in mind, a target percentage of end users that should end up regularly using a dashboard, and acting on the insights therein. Is there a critical mass, or percentage, that must be achieved in order to reach the intended outcomes? Initially there will be some trial and error, but this type of target will become the linchpin of any and all data efforts that seek to move the needle for the business.

11

Training and documentation

STORY

I used to be a fan of documentation. I do not mean I enjoyed writing the documentation, far from it, but I liked the notion of having well thought out and detailed guidance for getting users up to speed on how to use the dashboard and its various details. Probably a surprise to no one but myself, it turned out that most people did not enjoy reading lengthy documentation.

That sentiment surfaced one time when I overheard a client joking with a colleague about the 100+ page training document I had created for them, saying something along the lines of needing a few spare hours in their day to figure out how to use the training materials, yet alone the dashboard! While my sensitivities were affected, the message was heard loud and clear.

I went and had some candid conversations with past clients and asked if they had received good feedback on the documentation that went along with their insights. By and large, the sentiment was positive on having extensive documentation, but most felt they were underutilized and thought having an accompanying "quick start guide" type of document would be advantageous as the main document was unwieldy.

As with many other aspects of the process, there were already best practices to explore that might lend application to the data and BI space. There is no shortage of wonderful approaches to training and enablement. Incidentally, after researching and adapting them, this also opened up the world of training and public speaking to me.

For some, training and documentation is no fun. Oftentimes it is not conducted at all, and when it is the predominance of the content is simply screenshots with a few ill-formed steps and guidance to fill up the pages. However, when applied correctly, training can transform adoption and be a considerable accelerator to change management efforts.

A successful application of training will increase user trust and comfort with the new dashboard. It will help them become familiar with the interface and what it can do for them. Training presents an opportunity to convey the benefits of the insights and to make them relatable to the end users. Of course, training would also tell them how to use the interface. It would span where the data is coming from, what are the metric definitions, how the KPIs are calculated, and what the visualization means. In addition, specifically for this process, there must be an intuitive way of finding out what actions a dashboard drives and what the desired outcomes are for leveraging the interface.

There is much to do, even after the heavy lift of development, where a large portion of time is spent in respect of the overall process. With a thumb-in-the-air estimation, completing the development phase of the process is roughly 60 percent of the way to the end of the iteration. With the expectations of the team set accordingly, the appropriate time should be allocated to training. The party is only just getting started after development! Training is fun, especially in devising ways of how the end users can consume it.

Training, as it fits into the process outlined in this book, is a discrete step that is completed once the development outputs are ready to go into production. It takes its place here as the bulk of the training content will be based on the prior three phases: requirements, design, and development. However, it does not just begin after development. As will be covered in this chapter, training should be integral to the design stage and only be finalized after the development stage.

Busy people, no time

A major obstacle that any training program faces is the availability of the intended audience to consume the training. Gone are the days of hours-long training videos and extensive documentation. With the speed of information people are accustomed to and the hectic pace of business, people just do not have the time or attention to consume training in the traditional ways.

Just the notion of having to spend hours going through documentation to understand how a dashboard works is cause for frustration alone! The adage of "Sorry for the long letter, I didn't have the time to write a short one" applies well to training in the modern age. Training needs to be well thought out and easily consumable. It seems preposterous to expect people to work their way through a lot of training materials. However, much worse is no training materials at all! A balance needs to be struck between enough training to enable the user but not too much that it becomes overbearing to consume.

Just in time training

Just-in-time (JIT) training is delivered at the point when the user needs it. Not too far in advance and not after the fact. The idea comes from Toyota's well-known lean manufacturing approach, in which effort is expended if and when it is needed, and not before. For a learning application it means gaining new knowledge or skills only when needed, and not learning them if not needed.

With the proliferation of online training courses, access to knowledge and courses has become so easy that a person could wake up in the morning, decide they want to take a course on herbology, and have completed it by the evening. No lengthy process, ramp-up period, or communications are needed. It is learning on demand. However, that is self-actuated learning, which is slightly different from learning required to use an interface. Regardless of the differences, the pace of accessing the learning needs to be the same, i.e., where and when the consumer of the training wants it, and at a speed that the training does not become an activity in and of itself but is part of the activity.

A more traditional approach to training would be to set meetings with the end users to talk through how to use an interface. Basically, a classroom approach to teach how to use something. This approach can work well. The challenge can be when new people are onboarded and the classroom training is no longer available, i.e., it cannot be consumed without a trained facilitator. Modern training approaches, especially for the realm of BI, assume that training must be on demand and consumable in multiple ways in multiple formats. So, while there is much merit to classroom-based training for dashboard enablement, this book focuses on the modern approach of JIT training modalities.

The modern approach to user enablement

Ask any user experience designer worth their salt about user training and they will tell you one of two things. First, the preference is that the interface is so well designed that no training is needed to use it. The interface is intuitive enough that the user picks it up right away and is off to the races, as it were. Failing that, second, the training should be integrated into the user experience as much as possible. The user should not have to go to a separate interface to access the training to understand how to use the interface, especially if they do not know how to get to the training interface!

A very effective way to risk training failure is to introduce additional interfaces, more experiences that the user must navigate to accomplish their tasks. In the worst case, they may not be familiar with the training platform and may have to adjust to that before accessing the training they wanted in the first place. While there are definite advantages to consolidating all enterprise training on a single platform, training must still be accessible in the context of the user and not be a guessing game as to where to find it.

While it may be preferable, it can be a challenge to create a dashboard that requires no training. There are some scenarios where that would be possible, such as when users are already familiar with what to expect from a dashboard—for example, if several iterations have been completed, no new concepts are being introduced, and there are not expected to be any new users to the interface. It happens, but tends to be the exception rather than the rule.

In most cases there will be new users and new experiences that must be catered for. Occasionally, a new technology, such as a BI platform, may be introduced and extra attention will be needed to ensure a positive learning experience for both the introduction of new technology to experienced users, and the first-time users who are interacting with a dashboard on a new platform.

The modern approach is to minimize the distance a user must take to gain the knowledge they need. That means staying in the current interface and not navigating outside of it. The lower the friction, the better. Indeed, the experience should be seamless, whether performing the intended tasks in the dashboard or learning how to perform them. Modern BI platforms make this much easier with the advent of tooltips and in-context help.

Degree of user competence

Part of the benefit of taking the persona-based approach is the capability to also assess the competence of the intended audience, their technical ability, and their exposure to similar interfaces. This quick assessment can reveal what degree of training is needed and identify the gap that needs to be bridged in order for people to have a positive experience and efficiently perform the intended tasks in the dashboard. There can certainly be a range of experience, even within a single persona, so it becomes even more important to baseline the degree of training that will be needed to bridge the learning gap. The weakest link is the one that must be catered for.

Technology migrations can typically assume a similar baseline of lack of experience in a new tool, irrespective of the persona. For example, a report being moved from a spreadsheet over to a modern BI tool will need considerable training effort, and this may not be considered the responsibility of the team producing the new experience. The team may not have to train people in using a new platform, let alone take ownership of the training and design, and implement a training plan. So, it also raises the question of not just the user's competence but also the competence of the responsible team to deliver training for it. For these reasons, the training needs to be both easily consumable and easy to create.

It may seem obvious what training is, but sometimes the obvious is the first thing to be left behind. This can be especially true when timelines are tight. One of the first items to be slashed from a data project is training, and not necessarily because it is perceived as low value but perhaps because it is an activity that BI professionals are less comfortable with. Naturally, people prefer the activities they are educated and experienced to perform and, for folks in the data world, that usually does not include teaching people how to use an interface and get the most out of it.

Building and creating insights is the fun part! For many, teaching people how to use what has been built is less fun. There is a gap there. There is the thing that has been built, but not the knowledge handoff to those who need to use it optimally. However, that knowledge transfer is a key piece in the adoption puzzle and must take place if the promise of actionable insights is to be realized. No one else is going to create the necessary training materials, so it is down to the team building the dashboard to take ownership of enabling the end users in how to use what they have built. Therefore, it should be simple, quick to accomplish, and be manageable for people without a background in education.

Where should training happen?

Placing an emphasis on JIT training would strongly imply that the training material needs to be as close as possible to the dashboard, so it is available in the context of what the user is doing. To minimize the friction for the user and to maximize the likelihood that the training will be consumed, the training should be accessible directly in the dashboard.

Consider three scenarios for a user of a newly launched dashboard:

1 No training is provided
2 Training is available through the company learning portal
3 Training is available directly in the dashboard

In scenario one the user must figure out the new experience themselves. There are some questions they have about the calculations behind some of the KPIs but they are unable to find answers. They must resort to submitting a ticket to IT to ask what the definitions and calculations are. Perhaps they get lucky, IT is responsive, and they get a reply right away. However, the likelihood is that IT will either not know the answer or not get back in a timely manner because they are so overloaded with work. In a later session they want to know what the thresholds are for why one of the KPIs has gone red, but they do not bother to submit a ticket, so their question is unanswered and there is some doubt in their mind about the dashboard. Doubt that, if not addressed, could lead to a lack of trust and lower adoption.

In scenario two, the training is available, but it is in a different interface. If well executed, the individual knows how to access the training portal and can search by the name of the dashboard they want the training on. The challenge is that this type of training is not JIT, it is structured by a set of modules that the individual must wade through to find the answers to the questions they have. It is not a terrible situation, and is far more preferable to scenario one, but some users will not like it or have insufficient time to consume the material.

Scenario three places the training directly in the dashboard itself. The user can get the answers they want to specific KPIs they are interested in. There is no need to wade through content they do not have an interest in. There is a speed and efficiency to the experience and they only consume exactly what they need, when they need it. No waiting for IT, no jumping around to other systems, and no need to email colleagues for answers. They get what they need by their own hand. Not only is the user happier with this scenario but IT does not have to deal with the additional tickets! The benefits extend beyond the individual user experience. At scale, there can be significant time savings, reduced frustration, and more action can be taken from data.

Scenario three is clearly the preference. However, BI platforms are not built as training platforms and knowledge management systems. There is no need to do away with the training platform in scenario two, indeed, for some users, they might prefer to consume training in such a manner. A happy medium is to have both JIT training available in the dashboard but also have the more traditional training available in a learning management system or similar employee training portal.

Setting the context

Before any specific training can be delivered, the end user must first be brought up to speed about the dashboard, why it exists, and what questions it answers. This is especially true for the first time a user logs into a new dashboard. They should have answers to the following questions:

- Why was it created?
- What are the goals?
- Who is it for?
- What questions does it answer?
- What outcomes is it driving towards?
- Where does the data come from?
- Where can additional training materials be found?
- Who is responsible for the data?
- Who is responsible for the definitions, KPIs, and formulas?

All of these questions already have answers by consequence of following the process. There is no new information that must be determined, and the bulk of these answers are addressed by the strategy template. This gives the user tremendous context and purpose for what the dashboard can do for them. All of these details can be consolidated into one tab of a dashboard and this tab should be the default one that users see upon first usage. Just from this single tab the user knows where they need to go if they have questions; there are names and faces for the responsible parties as well as contact details. The proverbial black hole of support is dissolved. This tab engenders trust and comfort.

Not everything needs to be shown on a single tab, either. There could be multiple tabs in case fitting it all in one becomes too busy. It is vital information to give to the end user. It displays competence and business focus. Many of the typical questions that might be asked by a user initially can already be addressed with the overview tab. View an example of an overview tab on the book website.

Types of training content

With an understanding that extensive documentation, for training purposes, is not going to cut it by itself, what are the available types of training that can be delivered "just in time," within the constraints of a dashboard technology? The overview tab does a fine job of presenting the context and avenues for support, but it does not specifically show the user how the dashboard works. To do that, there are several media that can be leveraged within a dashboard to support training:

- training tabs
- video content
- links to training
- tooltips
- the help button

Training tabs

BI tools are not a replacement for a learning management system, and are not designed to be. Ideally, any training content that appears in a dashboard should also have a home in a proper company training portal or, at least, in a designated knowledge repository. Not all BI tools can support all the types of content that a training platform can, and certainly most will struggle with more advanced training aspects such as quizzes and tracking training progress. However, such advanced training features are not needed for the content that will make it onto the actual dashboard.

Like the overview tab, additional tabs can be used as a home for the training content that will be accessible from the dashboard. This is the philosophy of reducing the distance the user needs to travel in order to be enabled and quickly trained in the functionality and features of the dashboard. For some, a link to training on the overview tab may be sufficient. For others, it will be beneficial to have a training-specific tab they can view.

Imagine, as a user of the dashboard, opening it up for the first time. The first visual is the overview tab and all the context and objectives for the dashboard are made clear. Some high-level questions are addressed but there is more, as the training tab follows the overview tab in sequence. Clicking there presents a comprehensive set of training materials that can be quickly consumed. Just knowing it is there establishes a first port of call to check on, should any questions arise. It becomes the go-to tab for how to use the dashboard, regardless of whether the training content is directly embedded into the tab or linked to other systems.

Video content

The most obvious type of content, which is almost mandatory in modern training, is video. Short and to-the-point videos that help the user perform specific tasks. Lengthy videos are to be avoided as much as possible. Similar to pages and pages of documentation, a user should not have to jump around a video to find the part they are interested in. Videos should match closely the BVQ format and would be in the form of a question, such as, "How is gross margin calculated?" They should be in the form the user would ask the question if they were contacting support, i.e., natural language questions.

The production values do not need to be at a Hollywood grade. They need to be valuable and helpful before they need to be high quality. Just a glace at some of the most popular online videos provides ample evidence that value and entertainment beats quality. It is certainly a preference to have all three, where possible. By and large, the video format is screen recording with a voiceover. Video is very easy to capture these days and most operating systems already have screen recording software. It can be as simple as starting the video with the question the video is addressing and talking over it while recording how to answer it in the dashboard.

This type of training is very fast to produce and should remain so. Like much of the ideas in this book, simplicity must take priority. If it becomes too much of a burden, then people are less likely to create video content. There is no need for fancy effects, overlaid graphics, or any other visual embellishments. Additionally, a "talking head" does not need to appear on video so no webcam or camera equipment is necessary either. However, the microphone of the webcam may be used for capturing the voiceover instruction of the screen capture.

Video content can be directly embedded in the training tab and many BI platforms support video. Failing that, the video can be stored on the company knowledge platform and simply linked to from the training tab. Recording a video of the overview tab is a great place to start to set up the dashboard and add any additional color commentary as to why the dashboard exists and how it can help the end user.

Links to training

Video content is not intended to be a replacement for formal training materials. The challenge, of course, is that a BI platform is not the ideal place to host training materials. Providing external links to training for the dashboard is the next best option to having it directly embedded in the dashboard as there is only a short path for the user to take to access the training. There may also be existing training that the user needs to take that would be a waste of time to recreate, such as how to use the specific BI platform or technology that the dashboard is built on.

Regardless of the content, consolidating the links and references to training in one place is more than just a convenience for the user, it can be the difference between them using the dashboard or not. With such a focus on user enablement, users can spend their time on value rather than how to do things, and the difference is considerable. There are the unseen, unmeasured, hours of productivity wasted while people try to find what they need in the enterprise. Whether acknowledged or not, giving users that time back will only yield benefits to both the user and the business when applied at scale.

Tooltips

A tooltip is a box that appears when the cursor is placed over a certain visual element on an interface. For a dashboard, they can be activated over charts, KPIs, filters, and other elements of the interface. The tooltip is the linchpin of modern JIT training when it comes to dashboards. It provides smaller snippets of context for specific elements of the dashboard, as well as being able to provide bite-size chunks of training and knowledge.

Tooltips used to be very simple and just had the functionality of displaying text. Since then, they have evolved to be able to show a wide range of different media types from images and video, to even being able to embed some programmatic functionality such as conditional formatting based on what is going on with the data. They are at the point now, depending on the underlying BI technology, that they can be a primary means of user enablement and training delivery. In years past, they were a nice complementary piece of functionality to have. Nowadays, every dashboard strategy must have an approach for how to leverage them, in terms of both training and change management. Tooltips can provide a great depth of information when and where the user needs it. Users can ignore what they do not need and only consume the details they are interested in.

Consider hovering over a KPI in a dashboard. A tooltip pops up and displays how the KPI is calculated, what the data sources are for it, details on the KPI goal, the KPI target versus forecast, and historical performance. In addition, a description of the KPI would provide the rationale for why it is there and how it is tied to one or more strategic objectives. Any actions and behaviors it is designed to drive would also be addressed. It may even mention who was responsible for defining the KPI or providing a reference of where to find more information about it. This kind of coverage, just for a KPI, goes far above and beyond the traditional approach to reporting. It arms the end user with a wealth of information. Ideally, it is so complete that there is little need for the user to contact any others to get more detail. The beauty of it is that this information already exists; it has been gathered as part of the process. The tooltip is simply reflecting the outputs of the process in a consumable and accessible way for the user. This is not mere coincidence, but an important part of the process. All that detail must be transparent to the end user.

The utility of tooltips cannot be overstated. They do not even require a click to access, just a hover, a move of the hand. The user friction is incredibly low, and even the most demanding users will find benefit from the simplicity of access to any additional context they wish. However, this level of user experience is not a novelty, it is a requirement in order to match the consumer user experience. This level of convenience is also expected by the enterprise user. Recall the concept of a dashboard being a product that has a market. This market is made up of customers, and tooltips impact the customer experience. Indeed, to a degree, a type of passive customer service can be achieved by heading off the common questions that are addressable by tooltips and effective JIT training.

An even more important opportunity presents itself with tooltips. Actions. For every KPI and every chart, there are associated actions that come from the scenario mapping stage of the process. Tooltips become the store of actions and where they are quickly accessible by the end user. During the heat of the workday battle, they can be quickly found and acted upon, rather than having to dig through training materials and documentation or, indeed, just making things up on the spot. This is where the "So what?" is surfaced to the user and is the lever for enacting and shifting behavior towards the defined strategic goals. Again, this information already exists by following the process. It simply needs to be given life by being made accessible in a contextual format.

In summary, tooltips provide a compelling place to deliver bite-size chunks of context-relevant training, support, and knowledge. They are the Swiss Army utility tool for dashboard enablement.

The help button

More conventional training and help can be provided in the form of the ubiquitous help button: "?" It is a commonly understood visual element that tells the user that clicking it will bring up a dialog or a page that will provide help and support based on where they are in the interface. This is different from tooltips. Tooltips are chart- or visualization-specific elements that fall apart when the context becomes too broad. The help button, on the other hand, is at a higher level, usually relevant at the tab level and/or for the dashboard as a whole. It is where the more conventional, and searchable, help and training documentation can be found.

While video content is more digestible for many, this content provides a text-based alternative to the videos. It describes how the dashboard functions, what the tabs are, how the filters work, and the details of the functionality of the dashboard. Not least, it would cover what tooltips are and how to use them.

This type of training is not constrained by the limited space that is accorded to tooltips. Pages can be scrollable, can be indexed, reference other pages, and more. Not all BI platforms support this type of training content natively, but most can with plugins or additional modules. Alternatively, such training content could be placed in a scrollable tab in the dashboard that would be marked with a question mark icon.

Facilitated training

While JIT training is likely to be the most-utilized form of training, it can be appropriate to make live training sessions part of the change management experience. In such a way, the events are providing both a change management benefit in creating further awareness as well as the training benefit that users will know how the dashboard works before and during early usage of it. As these sessions tend to be longer in format, with participants sitting down, virtually or in-person, to attend the session, they need more planning and structure.

However, if planning and structure are barriers to running this type of training, an alternative is to run the session like a product demo. It would be a walk-through of the dashboard and how it works. The structure is created by the flow of the dashboard so requires less preparation than a formal training approach. For a demo, a suggested format would go like this:

1 Introduction to the dashboard

2 Step through the strategy template:

- objectives of the dashboard
- desired measurable outcomes
- who it is designed for
- important dates
- planned iterations and when to expect them

3 Open the dashboard

4 Review the overview tab

5 Cover where to find help and support

6 Address navigation

7 Progress through the tabs of the dashboard:

- the layout, and how KPIs, charts, and filters function together
- highlight the tooltip functionality

8 Walk through a scenario:

- a KPI turns red
- find more details in a chart
- explain how action works
- take the associated action

9 Summarize the dashboard and how to get support

10 Address any questions

Ideally, these sessions would be recorded so they can become part of the wider body of training materials and not one-off events that are lost in time. Considerable effort can go into creating facilitated training sessions, so it makes sense to capture them for on-demand use. The same goes for the more simplified demo format. There is nothing wrong with just recording these sessions with no attendees live! Indeed, it may be easier to complete, as scheduling is not a barrier, but the downside is that a potential change management opportunity and ability to field questions are lost. Depending on the scenario, those may be acceptable trade-offs or may not be relevant.

The importance of enablement

Empowered users more easily become advocates for change and can champion the adoption of a dashboard. Giving them all the tools to do this is a compelling strategy that will make future iterations and dashboards easier to release. The tactics covered in this chapter provide a suite of options that can be leveraged to support user enablement. However, enablement does not happen by itself, without some activating force, some event-based pressure. That is the domain of the launch, a set of steps to be triggered once the dashboard is ready for prime time.

12

Launch

STORY

When I decided to create my first product, the Dashboard Wireframe Kit, I had no idea how to launch it. Sales and marketing were out of my comfort zone and selling a physical product was not part of any experience I had. Not really knowing how to approach it, I turned to the experts. As it happens, there is an entire platform dedicated to launching products, called Kickstarter. Kickstarter has a step-by-step process for launching a product and, not being a fan of reinventing the wheel, I decided to follow their approach.

It was very detailed, with many examples and case studies to reference. I felt much better that many people had travelled the same path I wanted to take. Even better was that there were discrete steps I could follow to do it. That was a great start but, as I was to find out, there were other approaches out there. Through my research, I came across Jeff Walker, the author of the Product Launch Formula. His approach taught me that there really is a formula to launching a product. In effect, it is a very efficient means of maximizing the potential for people to buy your product.

By mixing the various approaches, some trial and error, lots of error actually, I found an approach that works for BI and analytics. It was only by going through the process of launching a physical product myself that I could see how important it is to have a similar launch sequence in the enterprise that could support the adoption of dashboards.

STORY

Aiden, a door-to-door salesman, knocks on the door of a large house in an affluent neighborhood. After a while, Athena opens the door. Athena is a little frustrated by the intrusion as she was about to start filming a new episode of her management consulting guide. Unaffected by Athena's obvious disdain, as Aiden introduces himself he seems a little distracted by what appears to be going on behind Athena. Annoyed, Athena looks around but sees nothing and asks what is up. Aiden seems to struggle with whether he should say it or not but comes out with it that, for such a wonderful home, it looks a little messy.

Athena is about ready to close the door when Aiden makes a comment that it explains why Athena looks a little tired. Somewhat aghast at the audacity of this guy, Athena says that, yes, she has been having trouble sleeping, but not because of the house being a little unclean! Or maybe it is? Aiden can see he has a hook and elaborates that Athena is obviously a very busy and successful person and how life is a series of trade-offs. Do you focus on career and family at the neglect of hobbies, personal interest, or even a clean house? He discusses the downsides of not having a clean house, like not feeling comfortable having people over to visit. The house is so expensive and beautiful it seems like a missed opportunity to not be living the social life you could.

Athena is finding something oddly compelling about what Aiden is saying— there is some truth to it. As Aiden continues to paint such a wonderful picture, Athena starts to wonder if this is the missing piece in the life of her family? Could it possibly be that, subconsciously, the unrealized dreams of having a vibrant and engaging social ensemble in their home is what is keeping her from having restful sleep? Probably not, but maybe?

Aiden presses on and talks about how different life would be for the kids to have parents that are more relaxed and happier. Everyone knows a happy family leads to better outcomes and not just for the kids, but for careers too! Somehow, magically, Aiden is able to throw out some statistics in support of this wild conversation that, by pure happenstance, must have veered way off the intended path. One study cites an increase in productivity of those that work from home of 20 percent when they do not have to worry about the state of their home. Yet another explores how a vibrant home that regularly has visitors over triples the odds of the household kids getting into an Ivy League college.

On some level it all makes sense, there are even studies to prove it, but all this is somewhat unhelpful for Athena as she would have to sacrifice other aspects of her life in order to have more time to spend on the house. With a curious look on his face, Aiden throws out a question. What would Athena pay per week to have the outcomes from the studies? Having a background in finance, Athena estimates the long-term impact of what being 20 percent more productive would mean to her career. She comes up with $200 per week. By sheer coincidence, Aiden has an artificial intelligence cleaning robot that can be leased for as little as $99 per week! But he only has one left because everyone else in the neighborhood got one already. The neighbors just got theirs 30 minutes ago and are already elevating their lives. Athena signs on the spot.

Problem, agitate, solve

Launching a dashboard is almost entirely aligned to selling a product. Therefore, why not adapt the best practice approach to sales to ensure greater adoption? The fun scenario in the story of Aiden and Athena relays one of the oldest approaches in the sales playbook: problem, agitate, and solve, or PAS for short. First, the problem must be identified and understood. Second, the problem is agitated. Finally, a picture must be painted of what the solution looks like.

In the example, Aiden identified the problem of the house not being spotless. He agitated it by linking lack of sleep to the problem. Not being one to just make problems worse, he presented a solution after envisioning what life could be like if that problem were solved. Athena went on a journey that was a little like a rollercoaster. She started out angry at having to talk about a major pain point, the dirty house. She connected another problem she had, lack of sleep, to this foundation and causal problem. She was then uplifted by envisioning what life might be like if the problem was solved and was even able to place a value on it. She was ready to buy after seeing the contrast between what life was like in the present versus what it would be like once all the benefits of solving the problem were realized.

This is a proven way to sell. The challenge, unfortunately, is that the days of being able to keep someone's attention for that length of time, to bring them on that journey, are gone, by and large. However, the formula is still valid. What needs to change is how the story is delivered. Rather than one single, but long, engagement, it can be distributed across several shorter interactions. But that is not enough. There are some other triggers that play into why the salesperson example works. It is timebound in that the person is only at the door for a moment in time, so there is an urgency to it. There is also rapport and trust being built during the longer interaction. There is a sense of scarcity created because Aiden only had one left. Finally, and perhaps most importantly, there is social proof. If the neighbors got one, Athena must get one too.

All these aspects can be mapped into a launch sequence for any kind of product, not least a dashboard. Whether people adopt a dashboard depends on how well the dashboard has been sold to them. Increasing adoption often involves influencing the decision of the intended target audience. Mental triggers can be powerful levers to use in service of that goal. A mental trigger is a proven means of influencing behavior and decision-making. Jeff Walker, in his book *The Product Launch Formula*, cites them as:

- scarcity
- social proof
- trust
- authority
- reciprocity
- anticipation
- likeability
- events/rituals
- community

While all of them offer something of value, the first two are particularly important for the purposes of increase adoption of insight in the enterprise.

Scarcity

People are less likely to buy when there is an abundance of something. A natural preference is to put off making a decision if there is no compelling external force. If they feel like they have all the time in the world, they will put off the purchasing decision. There needs to be a limited time and/or a limited quantity to produce a sense of urgency. It is why Black Friday exists—a window of time to grab the best deals all year, but the stock is limited! That limited opportunity sells vast amounts of merchandise. Kickstarter follows the same principle. They set a fixed amount of time for a project to be funded and, often, most of the funding happens in the last hours of a campaign because the time is running out—get in now or there will not be any other opportunity to buy.

The fear of missing out (FOMO) can have a part to play here in why the scarcity trigger works. FOMO is the feeling or perception someone can have that other people are having a better experience than they are, that they are missing out on a potential opportunity. "What if my colleagues don't have to manually compile multiple spreadsheets anymore but I'm still doing that?"

For a dashboard, it can mean running a pilot, prior to the formal launch of the dashboard, where only a limited number of people will get access to the dashboard. The bonus is that they will also be able to give direct feedback and have their inputs prioritized for the next iteration. Since it is timebound, the date becomes an anchor point for people to remember. There is a sense of scarcity created and only those in the pilot will get ahead of their colleagues to realize the promised benefits that the dashboard delivers.

In instances where a pilot does not make sense, perhaps there is a very small user base, or the speed of iteration is very fast, scarcity can still be in play by giving feedback priority to those who log into the dashboard the most in the first week of the launch. There are many avenues open to activate the scarcity mental trigger.

Social proof

People are more comfortable to do something if there are others doing it. The more people, the greater the influence. There is a desire to fit into society and to be accepted by one's peers. The more that people "like" something, the better it must be! When shopping online, if two products do the same thing but one has 1,000 five-star reviews and the other has 100,000 five-star reviews, people are more likely to buy the one with more reviews. There is much more social proof.

Ratings, reviews, and comments play a huge role in influencing purchasing decisions. Reading stories about how a certain product changed the life of someone or improved their situation can help the potential buyer imagine what that transformation might look like for them. They can envision what life would be like with the product with their burden lifted.

Seeing other people do something can also compel action in others to do the same thing. Especially if that action is novel in some way. People are more likely to act in the new way if they are not the first to do it.

Imagine a new dashboard is being launched and, prior to the launch, an email is sent as a reminder that the launch is imminent. In that email is a picture of Maria, a colleague. Beside her picture is a quote from her that reads:

> I was initially skeptical about the claims the team was making about what these insights could do for me. They had thrown out some pretty wild numbers, like I would be able to save four hours a week of manual spreadsheet work and would have more time to focus on the things that our company cares about, such as hitting our KPIs. Honestly, when they first announced the dashboard was in the works, I replied to their email saying I didn't think they were being honest. Well, they invited me to be a beta user of the dashboard and I got early access to it about two weeks ago. What can I say? Gone are the days of manual data entry and stitching my spreadsheets together! Since I do a lot of reporting, I can honestly say I got back eight hours in my week and can focus on the KPIs at the top of the dashboard. I'm actually making decisions with the data now rather than spending a chunk of my time just getting it into shape!

People that match Maria's persona will resonate with this, especially if she has a similar role and title to them. The more testimonials, the better. In addition, and even better, would be if Maria were available for a live question-and-answer session after this email. She could talk through the benefits to her in more detail and help potential new users to feel more comfortable with the new experience.

The offer

Any great product has an offer. What does the buyer get in exchange for the time, effort, and/or money? There must be an exchange of value. Fortunately, that is already documented throughout the process, but it must be appropriately packaged into a digestible format. The launch sequence is the delivery framework for the offer and the vehicles are email, video, messages, and even internal blog posts.

The consumer is inundated with offers all the time. From credit card deals that arrive in the mail to limited time discounts on an anti-virus software, there are a mass of offers. It is an experience that people are used to, but it is underleveraged in the enterprise to help increase adoption. The offer in the above example was that Athena could transform her life and that of her family for only $99 a week. For a dashboard, as an example, a sales professional end user could be able to increase their sales commissions by $1,000 a month if they invest four hours a week with the dashboard. Whatever the offer is, it must be made clear what the user gets for their investment.

The launch sequence

Launching a dashboard is more than just granting permissions and access to the intended users. Much like the change management approach, it requires careful thought and does not happen in just one step—it is realized over the course of the dashboard creation lifecycle and will leverage many of the assets created along the way. The launch sequence takes place over three phases. These are the pre-launch, the launch, and the post-launch.

The pre-launch involves communication with the end users, letting them know that a new dashboard is coming their way in the future. These communications would inform them what the dashboard is all about, what it will do for them, and when can they expect it. Of particular importance is emphasizing the transformation it is intended to deliver to them and the benefits it will create. If this is done early enough, there may be the opportunity to ask for volunteer pilot users, who will have early access to the dashboard and give their feedback. The pre-launch would also entail the creation of any of the communication assets that are needed. Samples of these communications are available on the book website. They include emails, event invitations, agendas, videos, and posters, in some cases. Before the dashboard is going to be available, the intended audience should be made aware it is coming and what they can expect from it. The intent of the pre-launch is to prime the audience for what is coming and to make them eager and excited that it is on the way. The pre-launch must include the offer.

The climax of the launch stage happens after development is complete. Where the pre-launch builds anticipation, the launch delivers on the promise. The launch should be anchored to the specific date on which people will be able to access the dashboard. Of course, all the necessary permissions and access should be in place. It would be a very poor user experience to have heard so many good things about a new dashboard but then, on launch day with lots of fanfare, it cannot be accessed, and a support ticket needs to be sent. Ideally, launch day should have an associated event. When Apple first launched the iPod, there was much anticipation and excitement, and the event did not disappoint.

The launch event could be something as simple as a virtual demo of the new dashboard that would be kicked off with the appropriate context and background. To make sure people stick around to the end, they can be enticed to stay by giving something special away at the end of the event. Whatever the event is, it must clearly be understood when it is happening, and the necessary stakeholders and end users are aware of it.

The post-launch is all about delivering a positive customer service. People may have a range of problems, such as losing their credentials, browser challenges, and dashboard-specific items, even if they are addressed in the training and enablement content. Some users will not look at any documentation and will need some extra attention to get them on board. The end user must have a differentiated customer experience from end to end of the process, so they are willing and eager for future iterations and other dashboards.

The next iteration

The launch sequence extends the dashboard as a product concept from the start of the process and seeks to sell the product at the end of the process, bringing it to a natural conclusion. A product unsold is a wasted product. The launch step makes sure all the value and effort that went into the previous steps is maximized and realized by the target market. Wrapping up an iteration in this way will have many happy users and plenty of opportunity to gather more social proof and people eager to give feedback for the next iteration.

Due to all this work, the lift on the subsequent iteration is lighter. The strategy template should be re-visited and tweaked, but not started anew. A new persona may be introduced but the stakeholders are likely constant. The KPIs can be reviewed, potentially re-prioritized, and amended but there is already plenty to go off. The data assessment is a lighter lift as there is already a degree of understanding from the prior iteration. Wireframes can be extended, but the layout and structure are already established. Development is iterated upon, but many of the data connections are in place. Finally, the launch and adoption stages become easier and start to yield more results with each subsequent iteration.

Parting advice

The ideas in this book are useless without application. They do not need to be applied wholesale, but there are very likely elements that have been presented that would make a difference and not be too difficult to try out. If low adoption is a problem, and it has not been remedied to date, it is likely more harmful to continue along the path of low adoption than it is to stumble and fumble a few times while trying out a potential solution.

Start small, maybe on a dashboard for a small number of users—five to ten is a safe range. Get their feedback and thoughts. How can it be improved? What worked and what did not land? Most importantly, just get started. The biggest blocker is just taking that first step. That first step is made a lot easier by being armed with the right set of tools. The fastest way to do that is to visit the book website and download all the templates and accelerators that are mentioned in the book. Just showing up at work with these tools will turn some heads and put people on notice that something new is on the horizon. In lieu of experience and confidence with the process, lean on the tools and start today!

INDEX